BRAND CHAMPIONS

BRAND CHAMPIONS

How Superheroes Bring Brands to Life

Ian P. Buckingham

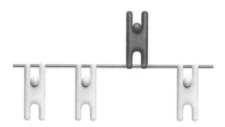

bring yourself 2 work

palgrave
macmillan

First published 2011 by
PALGRAVE MACMILLAN

Palgrave Macmillan in the UK is an imprint of Macmillan Publishers Limited, registered in England, company number 785998, of Houndmills, Basingstoke, Hampshire RG21 6XS.

Palgrave Macmillan in the US is a division of St Martin's Press LLC, 175 Fifth Avenue, New York, NY 10010.

Palgrave Macmillan is the global academic imprint of the above companies and has companies and representatives throughout the world.

Palgrave® and Macmillan® are registered trademarks in the United States, the United Kingdom, Europe and other countries.

ISBN 978–0–230–22032–4

This book is printed on paper suitable for recycling and made from fully managed and sustained forest sources. Logging, pulping and manufacturing processes are expected to conform to the environmental regulations of the country of origin.

A catalogue record for this book is available from the British Library.

A catalog record for this book is available from the Library of Congress.

10 9 8 7 6 5 4 3 2 1
20 19 18 17 16 15 14 13 12 11

Printed and bound in Great Britain by
CPI Antony Rowe, Chippenham and Eastbourne

For Holly Boo and the Mighty Atom!

"I don't wanna be in a band, I wanna be in a brand."
(Gene Simmons, formerly Chaim Witz, better known as
his tongue-flicking, blood-spitting alter ego
"Demon" and bass player in KISS)

"He who fools with the brand must surely be burned."
(Xhosa proverb)

CONTENTS

LIST OF FIGURES

INTERBRAND'S TOP TEN BRANDS IN 2009

1.	Coca-Cola	68,734 ($mn)
2.	IBM	60,211 ($mn)
3.	Microsoft	56,647 ($mn)
4.	GE	47,777 ($mn)
5.	Nokia	34,864 ($mn)
6.	McDonald's	32,275 ($mn)
7.	Google	31,980 ($mn)
8.	Toyota	31,330 ($mn)
9.	Intel	30,636 ($mn)
10.	Disney	28,447 ($mn)

WHAT BRAND LEADERS SAY

"We have a clearly defined brand mission, vision, and values. Authenticity plays a vital role here ... It builds trust and credibility with the consumer and provides the basis for identification with your brand, and it must never be jeopardized."

Erich Stamminger, adidas group

"The importance of brand coherence across geographic boundaries and across internal and external audiences contributes to building a successful brand."

David Bickerton, BP

"In my experience, simplicity has always been entirely more effective than complex brand development and communication, so a robust, authentic strategy is always better than an over-engineered and some-what aspirational approach."

James Leipnik, Canon

"Next to our employees, the brand is our company's most important immaterial asset, and protecting its value is of great importance to everyone at Siemens."

Michael Rossa, Siemens

(All of the above featured on the Interbrand website – Interviews with global brand leaders)

PART 1

WHAT'S A CHAMPION BRAND?

A brand is simply a promise of value provided by a product, a service or an organization. It's an asset which creates differentiation and can generate superior returns. Champion brands make compelling, sustainable promises to the market. What makes them different is that they do this only after they have developed an engaging internal culture where employees keep those promises. They then work hard at sustaining that culture through authentic employee engagement. As the best brand managers know, you simply can't keep your promises to customers unless you keep your promises to your staff. If you've already read *Brand Engagement* and you're now reading this, you presumably agree with the core hypothesis that brand management, as the route to sustaining superior returns, is an increasingly important professional discipline and that great brands are primarily built from within.

The overwhelming weight of brand management collateral in the market still prioritizes external stakeholder engagement. Of course the externally focused brand valuation criteria used by the companies which compile the branding charts mean that these brand beauty parades which have helped to establish brand management as an essential element of corporate strategy are very much reserved for the global mega brands, the branding top table. But they shouldn't be disregarded by the vast flotillas of smaller organizations. There are still essential, holistic brand truths to be gleaned from these brand beauty parades. The existence of an elite league certainly doesn't mean that organizations, regardless of size, sector or constitution, can't access or even contribute to the great brand best practices even if the smaller players will never make it onto the lists.

A quick glance at quotes from global brand leaders such as those featured opposite from the likes of Siemens, Canon and adidas hints

1

at the core elements of brand management best practice. These core elements include:

- valuing the brand as highly as you value your employees
- ensuring the brand strategy is simple and the brand is:
  - recognizable
  - trustworthy
  - seen as a signifier of origin
  - a promise
  - functional
  - emotional
- keeping the engagement strategy authentic or real
- ensuring brand coherence internally and externally
- having a clearly defined and synergistic vision, mission and values
- maintaining the trust of all stakeholders

There are still those who decry the notion of brand management and question the relevance of the brand to employees. But these are all principles that can be applied to any organization with customers to cater to and with employees to embody and bring its brand to life in the face of those customers.

In *Brand Engagement,* I made the case for building great brands first and foremost from within, by engaging employees with the brand development journey *before* attempting to engage external stakeholders. The invention of the term "internal marketing" may have helped to lend credibility to internal communication in the very early days. But times have changed, and internal marketing is now a counterproductive misnomer. As a former director of two Omnicom companies and therefore well versed in the marketing, communications and design worlds, I urge organizations to face up to the reality that employees are a very different and much tougher stakeholder group than customers and to prioritize brand management from the inside out rather than attempting to corral, align and conscript staff using the same marketing mentality they apply to their customers.

It really is ludicrous that the internal or promise-keeping community still receives so little acknowledgment from the marketing professions. They really are missing a trick. *Marketing Week*, for example, as recently as June 17, 2010, in an article on re-branding sourced from Rebrand. com titled "Top 10 Mistakes Marketers Make When Rebranding – and How to Avoid Them" mentions thinking beyond the logo and stationery, considering existing goodwill, doing the research and so on. But there's absolutely no mention of the importance of employees and no attempt to point out the need to consult and engage with them. It makes no sense whatsoever.

Communication budgets, whether cloaked in the trappings of advertising spend, PR or even internal communication, are too precious to waste on empty promise-making without ensuring that the promise keepers, the employees, are willing and able to deliver. Internal marketing and internal communication, however, are not the same thing. The communication techniques used to engage external audiences are not entirely transferable to internal audiences.

Without, of course, wishing to dissuade anyone who hasn't yet made the investment in the prequel, it may be helpful at this stage to give a brief ten-point summary of my own, setting out the key themes from *Brand Engagement*:

1. High profile, hero leaders are, of course, important figures in the brand management process. But it's the *chief engagement officers*, the workaday everymen within organizations, who are primarily responsible for internal brand engagement (more ceo and less CEO).
2. The brand doesn't reside in the marketing department. It isn't the logo. It isn't distinct from the organization. It is the organization; it's the sum of *promises made less promises kept*.
3. To manage the brand effectively, it's essential to have a close working relationship or collaborative partnership between the triumvirate of *CEO's office, Marketing and HR,* traditionally the custodians of the internal and external promise-making parts of the business.
4. Brand development activity needs to be expressed as part of an *ongoing narrative*, a story that respects the legacy of the brand and engages all stakeholders with the future.
5. The *vision, mission, values and behaviors* absolutely need to be reflected in the brand, and the brand management process should be an integral part of business strategy.
6. It's at least as important to develop an *appropriate internal culture*, reflecting and sustaining the brand, as it is to attract customers to it.
7. Brands are approximately *80% behavioral and 20% physical,* and brand management budgets should reflect this.
8. Brand *engagement* takes place predominantly at an *emotional level* rather than a rational one, and internal communication needs to

respect and reflect this not attempt to align employees and force compliance with rational guidelines.

9. *Authenticity* is the cornerstone of brand survival, and employees are far more sensitive to and intolerant of insincerity than customers.

10. Brands are arguably filling in for traditional *sense-making* institutions like the state and religion as sources of identity and higher order needs, thereby affording brand development increasing importance.

The good news is that each of the ten points or brand development milestones detailed above can be readily acted upon provided the brand is acknowledged by the top team as a key driver of value. Importantly, with the right people leading the process, a comprehensive brand engagement program shouldn't need a substantial budget. This is especially encouraging in leaner times.

Despite substantial, across the board cuts in employee engagement related spending throughout 2008/09 in the US and UK, which is sadly still seen as discretionary spending, advertising spend was reported by Kantar Media to be $31.3bn in the first three-quarters of 2010 in the US alone. Imagine the opportunity cost of wasted marketing spend in general when it isn't supported by employee behavior. Now imagine the potential income-generating opportunities that could stem from reversing this logic.

The more frustrating news for the assiduous gatherer of best practices is that there isn't a common magical route map to follow in terms of how the leading brands became great. You can pick up tips but can't just copy what Disney does. Their magic dust is unique. Developing your own approach to change is more engaging and a lot more fun.

The approach McDonald's takes is as different from Google's as the journey taken by Apple is from that of Microsoft. Leading brands do, however, share the majority of the core principles and philosophies.

Most importantly, however, when brand development is properly prioritized and the values placed at the core of the strategy, the outcomes are always the same:

- engaged stakeholder communities
- enviable financial metrics

It's these two factors existing in harmony – particularly engaged employees or colleagues within the stakeholder communities – that make brands great, that create champion brands.

4

FOUR STEPS TO BRAND ENGAGEMENT

The route taken along the internal brand engagement journey is unique to individual corporate cultures but it essentially has four common stages/steps, which are explored at length in the prequel:

Step 1 Developing the business case for brand engagement (the why?)

- brand valuation
- leadership conviction
- collaboration between HR and Marketing to develop cost/income metrics, cost of nonconformance, opportunity cost and so on
- development of unique brand balanced scorecard including behavioral and process related brand metrics
- inclusion in business strategy and sharing with line management as SMART goals

Step 2 Creating brand awareness

- clarifying the brand in physical *and* behavioral terms
- creation of context by crafting the story of the evolution of the business and brand
- development of change roadmap
- development of internal communication strategy
- communication of the behavioral aspects of the brand (principles, values and behaviors)
- focus on line managers/ceos
- communication of the strategy
- highlighting brand champions to reinforce positive behavior
- internal brand and culture audit

Step 3 Achieving brand engagement

- implementation of culture development strategy
- values and behaviors engagement initiatives (giving people the chance to "play")
- implementation of pan-channel communication strategy
- moving communication from push to pull

- numbers of initiative-taking brand advocates and champions increasing
- all people processes in sync with brand

Step 4 Maintaining brand commitment

- measurement (staff and customer related) against the brand balanced scorecard
- behavioral reinforcement via people processes
- sustaining innovation and self-managing teams
- brand advocate numbers dominate
- reflection, continuous improvement and reset horizons
- communicating/celebrating best practices and use of appreciative inquiry

I have given and continue here to give a range of examples of organizations that have transformed their brands from the inside out by hitting each of the milestones detailed above. They don't necessarily arrive at the milestones in the order set out but they have, during the journey, greatly improved the valuation of their brand as an asset; have often made it into the Best Companies polls; have excelled during other stakeholder assessments and in each case have greatly improved their bottom line. The great brands don't judge success by shareholder perceptions alone.

The aim of this sequel to *Brand Engagement* is to get further inside admired brands and share some of the stories of the people who are undoubtedly engaged with their successful brands and who bring their brands to life through their everyday actions. It is to help organizations recognize the power of engaged employees and the importance of creating advocates across the *4 C's of The Engaging Organization*:

Communities – corporate and social responsibility, including sustainability

Customers and Consumers – external communication; the organization and its brands

Colleagues – past, future and present employees

Corporate – governance and reporting for financial markets, investors, analysts, journalists, value and supply chain; collaboration with suppliers and partners as measures of the ability to work and communicate across silos and boundaries

Given that the target readership includes a wide range of people who are interested in brand management, this book doesn't always feature intimidating superhero organizations from an Interbrand-style Best 100 Brands poll with equally impressive PR machines of their own. Having worked across industries in this field for some time, my intention is to make the case for the workaday Everyman as brand champion, whether they work for an FTSE 100 company or family business. I've highlighted a variety of brand champions, wherever they may be found, with whatever brand they are comfortable to bear on their breast. Having had the privilege to work with many of the people featured here, my aim is to share some of the insights and best practices that have shaped what I consider to be champion brands from the perspective of the little people who make admired brands what they are. Whatever your reason for picking up this book, there should be insights that you can apply.

WHAT'S A BRAND CHAMPION?

Of course I have a secret identity. I don't know a single superhero who doesn't. Who wants the pressure of being super *all the time?*

Mr. Incredible

Of course, it isn't only children who dream of being heroes when they grow up. Even as so-called grown-ups we cling onto the belief that we can earn the respect and admiration of our peers. I happen to agree with J.M. Barrie and like-minded writers, philosophers and even psychologists who suggest that we never really grow up, just learn how to behave in public. Who hasn't daydreamed at work about doing heroic things, whether it's returning victoriously from a pitch meeting, helping a colleague thrive or slaying a "dragon" of a boss who has terrorized colleagues for years?

Ask a group of people what comes to mind when they hear the word "champion" and the list is likely to include terms such as "winner," "protector," "leader" and so on. The qualities of champions will inevitably include terms such as "courage," "bravery" and "skill." Invariably, however, a true champion will be seen to be acting on behalf of others, sacrificing part of themselves for a greater cause.

So how come the term "champion" leaves something of an unpleasant, "corporatized" aftertaste when used in a business context?

FIGURE 1   **Mural on a school playground wall**

Perhaps the answer lies in the way the "experts" define the term. For example, in their blog *Brand Strategy (*http://www.brandingstrat egyinsider.com/2006/08/characteristics.html) Day and VanAuken offer the following:

Characteristics of Successful Brand Champions

Chief brand champions will be more effective if they exhibit the following personal characteristics:

- *Curious*
- *Well rounded*
- *Intuitive*
- *Visionary*
- *"Big picture" thinker*
- *Strong customer knowledge*
- *Strong business knowledge*
- *Assertive*

- *Disciplined*
- *Tenacious*
- *Resilient*
- *Passionate*
- *Able to simplify the complex*
- *Able to translate brand concepts into something relevant for nonmarketers*
- *Storytelling ability*
- *Teaching ability*
- *Likable personality*

A rather exhaustive and intimidating roll call of traits for the so-called "chief brand champion" or CBC which could equally be applied to many customer-facing functions, even if they do break down into three implied roles:

(1) vision crafter (2) teacher/evangelist and (3) standards enforcer

I can see how this wish list is desirable within the hallowed halls of the C suite. But how achievable is it? Some brand champions, like Bill Gates, may be "vision crafters" but can he also be said to "enforce standards"? Isn't a brand champion more of an inspirational figure than an auditor; more leader than manager; more explorer of brand potential than policeman of brand guidelines; more behavioral than process driven?

I've seen a host of similarly demanding definitions ranging from *"an employee of an organization who is responsible for the development, performance and communication of a particular brand"* through to the rather more creative *"internal and external storytellers who spread the brand vision, brand values and cultivate the brand in an organization."*

I particularly like the latter. It may run the risk of conjuring up images of quirky types in sandals irritating the workaday employee with talk and tales, but at least its engaging. I suspect, however, that the truth lies somewhere between these phlegmatic and fantastic extremes.

It's rather disingenuous to attempt to impose "champion" status on workers without understanding the cultural context relating to what society has deemed a champion to be. Achieving a common and acceptable definition inevitably means understanding the rich heritage of the champion genre in the storytelling tradition, which far predates corporate communication.

It was Joseph Campbell who, in the 1940s, first brought the mythic and archetypal principles embedded in the structure of stories to the public's attention. Interestingly, this was also the beginning of a golden age of advertising and a time when the superhero genre was at its height.

In *The Hero with a Thousand Faces*, Campbell identified the underlying patterns in cross-cultural myths, stories and spiritual traditions. He created a standardized language which made it possible to uncover and pass on the latent archetypal structure of these narrative traditions.

Christopher Vogler in *The Writer's Journey* took Campbell's work to the next stage by expanding on the language of the Hero's Journey, crafting it into a detailed framework for analyzing both plot and character development and into a guideline for developing satisfying and successful stories. Between them Campbell and Vogler helped us understand the storytelling patterns which are programmed in each of us. They highlight communication norms, an unwritten sequence of rules that we unconsciously apply to narrative regardless of whether it takes place in a corporate or informal environment. Campbell in particular created a set of cross-cultural rules by which champions are judged. If we apply this approach to corporate communication, especially change communication, the importance of the Everyman hero at the center of the story or narrative becomes clear.

THE CHAMPION AND THE HERO'S JOURNEY

Vogler breaks down Campbell's Hero's Journey, the journey of the Everyman as a metaphor for the journey of life, into 7 archetypes (the characters in the journey) and 12 stages or change milestones:

The archetypes

1. **Hero**: The Hero is the protagonist or central character. It is important that the Hero is essentially unassuming and unexceptional, even flawed in a way that encourages audiences to empathize with him.

   The Hero's primary role is to separate from the ordinary world and sacrifice himself for the service of the journey at hand – to answer the challenge, complete the quest and restore the ordinary world's balance. We experience the journey through the eyes of the Everyman Hero. We become engaged because we can relate to and sympathize with the Hero.

Our collective knowledge and experience of the Hero through our exposure to stories in our personal lives, regardless of format, establishes certain rules, rhythms, patterns and norms about the nature of the Hero, the qualities he possesses, the structure of the narrative journey and what the Hero must endure to earn the right to the title.

We instinctively apply these unconscious norms to any character in the social or corporate world to whom champion or heroic status is attributed. In short, heroic or champion status can't be bought; it must be earned.

Think Frodo Baggins, Erin Brockovich, Peter Parker/Spiderman or Dave Smith from accounts who steps forward to participate on the people panel during the Brand Refresh, or Sinead Maguire, a relatively junior member of staff who volunteered to interview the chairman and compere the all-staff conference at the Northern Ireland Tourist Board.

---

2. **Mentor**: The Mentor provides motivation, insights, experience and training to help the Hero, usually from the standpoint of experience. The Mentor stands for legacy, heritage and empowering knowledge.

Rob Woolley, former executive at CFS who coached their array of brand facilitators; the independent career coach; Batman's butler Alfred; Obi-Wan Kenobi; the trusted external consultant or coach; Jiminy Cricket; the right sort of bank manager or accountant; Professor Xavier; the ideal boss; Gandalf.

---

3. **Threshold Guardian**: Threshold Guardians protect the Special World and its secrets from the Hero, and provide essential tests to prove a Hero's commitment and worth.

> Executive personal assistants, the compliance department, the HRD, the Silver Surfer, Cerberus, the Head of Knowledge Management, procurement departments, the headhunter, the Minotaur; the Sirens.

4. **Herald**: Herald characters inject changes of pace and direction, issue challenges and announce the coming of significant change. They can make their appearance anytime during a journey, but often appear at the beginning of the journey to announce a Call to Adventure. A character may wear the Herald's mask to make an announcement or judgment, report a news flash or simply deliver a message. More often than not Chief Executives giving the "burning platform" address to employees inadvertently stray from mentoring or heroic status into the role of the Herald unless they are truly and appropriately engaging and personalize their approach.

> Head of Internal Communication, the MD's "back to the floor" visit, employee pulse take, Chairman, event facilitator, venture capitalists, Angel Gabriel, Finance Director, R2D2, Mr. Tumnus, spokesmen for customer focus groups or people panels.

5. **Shapeshifter**: The master/mistress of duplicity, insincerity and disingenuousness. The Shapeshifter's mask misleads the Hero by hiding a character's intentions and loyalties and deliberately diverting him from the path.

> Mystique (*X-Men*), Salome, self-promoting boss, networking competitor, Catbert the evil HR Manager, the serpent in the garden of Eden, Morgan le Fay.

6. **Shadow**: The Shadow represents our darkest desires, our untapped resources, or even rejected qualities. It can also symbolize our greatest fears and phobias. Shadows may not be all bad, and may reveal admirable, even redeeming, qualities. The Hero's enemies and villains often wear the Shadow mask, determined to destroy the Hero and his cause.

> The Eye and ring in *Lord of the Rings,* the cynical head of the management assessment center, the passive defensive colleague, the magic mirror in *Snow White*, the rogue recruitment consultant or sloppy intermediary, the raven in *Cinderella*.

7. **Trickster or Fool**: Tricksters relish the disruption of the status quo, turning the ordinary world into chaos with their quick turns of phrase and physical antics. The drama of the Fool springs from his free spirit, even if he is enslaved by a king as a court jester, by a domineering spouse or stuck in an all-day conference. Fools can be happy, sad, angry, clownish, outwardly frivolous, kind or cruel. They feel free to cross boundaries in thought or action and often reveal deep-seated truths through jest or mention the obvious things that others are afraid to confront. They can uncover other people's follies or they can bungle up their own worlds. They have unwritten license to manipulate, criticize, misjudge or tempt others due to the child still alive inside them. They can also yield to temptation more easily, opening the door to some serious drama.

Although they may not change during the course of their journeys, their world and its inhabitants are transformed by their antics. The Trickster uses laughter and ridicule to make characters see the absurdity of the situation, and perhaps force a change.

> Falstaff, the Joker, the Mad Hatter, Don Quixote, Pippin; Forrest Gump, the brand cynic, the team comedian or the cartoonist in the company magazine.

It's important to understand that Campbell wasn't inventing these archetypes. He simply, but painstakingly, identified and highlighted cross-cultural norms that we all instinctively recognize. Any initiative, whether brand development or otherwise, which deliberately or inadvertently references these stereotypes must demonstrate an understanding of the substantial body of lore from which they stem and the largely unwritten rules audiences apply as a result. Mentors, for example, have powerful social references which need to be recognized before implementing a formal mentoring program. The use of humor has legitimate and powerful, iconoclastic references throughout theatre and literature. But perhaps most powerfully of all, to call someone a champion implies a great deal about the status of the individual. True champions are representatives of their community and not necessarily of the establishment or governing cadre. They really need to be elected and not imposed.

Reflect for a second on the archetypes highlighted above. Consider who fulfils which role in your current team, the change management program team or the brand redevelopment process. Now consider the potential impact of helping people to switch roles or of finding people to reflect the archetypes that aren't currently represented to give the brand development story a greater sense of balance. For example, consider the impact of introducing an element of levity, comedy or play to a gathering or event, the license this gives for people to relax and speak the unspoken and how much more engaging the communication of key messages can be as a result. Or consider the role the nonexecutive Chairman can play; the introduction of an unexpected intervention or the binding effect of creating a common and alter ego enemy in the debate about strategy. These archetypes exist in the narrative structures we all have programmed into us. Why not recognize and use them during the engagement process?

Campbell's life's work tracked cross-cultural myths, legends and stories in an effort to reveal the inherent patterns and explain them. He deconstructed the stories inherent within societies. Given that the workplace is arguably the most important modern arena in which social interaction takes place, Campbell's teaching is extremely relevant to understanding organization culture, identity and the role of internal communication.

Having paused for reflection, you doubtless recognize a few of your own workmates past and present in the archetype descriptions given above. What does the list you've drawn up say about the strengths and weaknesses of that team and the nature of the dramas you generate and enact between you?

The most important point from a brand development perspective is that it is simply not possible to attribute champion or heroic status to any individual without understanding these unwritten "rules" and associated archetypes. To elevate an Everyman colleague to champion status implies that, in the eyes of their colleagues, whether they are conscious of it or not:

- they represent "us," the Everyman community
- the champion has undertaken some form of transformational journey during the course of their work and this has been for the greater good of the community
- they have encountered archetypes and have overcome trials and excelled for the greater good
- they have particular and unique insights to offer their community of origin (what Campbell calls "the elixir")
- they will ultimately be acting for the benefit of the community of origin

Simply sticking up a wall chart of star performers or sending out a newsletter with names handpicked by leaders who are probably out of touch with operational reality is counter-productive. It is unlikely to engage the wider colleague community and will probably alienate more people than it inspires.

Of course the alienated colleagues are unlikely to articulate their simmering resentment in an open way but they are going to question:

- why her?
- why now?
- they claim he/she's a champion but they're just a "fool/shadow" to me
- aren't they just doing a normal job?
- what's wrong with what I'm doing?
- who says they're better than I am?
- did I miss the nominations?

Not in so many words, but they are going to instinctively question whether the handpicked heroes are worthy of being singled out as champions; come to doubt the authenticity of the program they represent and whether the people highlighted aren't just another archetype in the brand development journey like (in whatever terms they choose) a threshold guardian (management flunkie), an insubstantial fool, a duplicitous shapeshifter and so on.

Even worse, if the majority of employees don't have a positive relationship with the organization and the official or establishment culture is at odds with the actual or established culture, a brand champions program is going to drive most employees into the shadows, "the underground resistance," instead. Here they will create a cynical subculture, and the so-called corporate brand champions will soon be ostracized by the community and lose any necessary influence. In the mythology surrounding Robin Hood, John may have been the king and the Sheriff of Nottingham his tax-collecting vassal, even brand champion, but it's clear that Richard and Robin were the true romantic heroes.

This scenario of officially sponsored brand champions at odds with the prevailing culture is a more common situation than you may think.

Consider the scenario outlined by Janet, an HR manager for a leading hotel chain, when I interviewed her in 2009:

Our Brand Ambassador program hit an all time low when someone vandalised the Employee of the Month Wall of Fame, drawing moustaches and horns on the staff photographs.

It was only after we held a series of independently hosted employee focus groups that we discovered how badly this initiative was being perceived by most staff.

It turned out they didn't trust our selection criteria; didn't understand why certain people were selected and others weren't; didn't buy into our version of what a brand champion should look like and were insulted that the awards implied that most of the staff were not performing as well as the people on the wall.

We've since turned the whole programme on its head and have recruited a cross-sectional team to revolutionise the program. They have created clear criteria linked to our brand values and stressing "selflessness" in particular and have created a weekly slot in team briefings where we all nominate colleagues who we believe have excelled that week. The team then write up pithy mini case studies once a month explaining learnings from the people featured.

The whole process has been democratized. As it's now owned by more people it's creating more of a buzz and has taken on a life of its own.

What Janet's tale reinforces is that heroes have to earn the title if they're to be accepted by the colleague community they are supposed to represent. If they don't, they're probably going to be associated with the tactics of managerial command and control. Key to their credibility and acceptance is establishing a set of standards related to the brand but recognized, respected and acknowledged by the wider community. This invariably involves consulting the wider colleague community from the "ordinary world" when establishing the standards which define a brand champion.

The champion and the journey

So:

- brand champions are made; they aren't born or appointed
- they need to represent the Everyman community
- it's important that there are many, not an elitist few

There is an implied rite of passage to achieving brand champion status, a change journey bridging the old brand culture and the aspirational culture. To become a champion you need to have experience, to be a role model, to walk the talk.

Campbell's Hero doesn't achieve heroic status, however, by sitting at home or remaining a "Steady Eddie." Campbell's notion of the Hero's Journey features the Everyman hero embarking on a transformational voyage of discovery during which he/she steps forward to undertake the trip and encounters a series of trials, threats and opportunities that constantly test the Hero's mettle. Sound familiar? If not then reflect on what the now glib but often repeated phrase "the only constant is change" actually means and what you're asking your colleagues to do differently when you trot out the phrase.

If you're highlighting issues with the brand and asking people to do something different, to change the way they work, that difference is going to have to be placed in context if people are going to commit to change. Sure, leaders can force people to do things differently or do different things in the short term. But sustaining that change is another matter. Hiring mercenaries to act on short-term orders for immediate gain is one thing. Creating a self-managing and innovative, engaging, sustainable culture is another.

If the ideal brand champion is an Everyman representative of the ordinary organization world, then their journey represents the change process necessary to transform the brand. The milestones become the brand development program.

In corporate land, change is too often depicted as an unemotional and dry task for pragmatic project managers. The reality for those who experience it is very different.

Campbell's model can work well as a more engaging way of placing people, heroes and corporate archetypes alike, within the change narrative. It can be a way of understanding and plotting the milestones along the journey that are necessary to achieve and embed lasting change. It's a lot more fun and a deal more inspiring than a Prince II Gantt chart pinned to the wall of the project "war room" for people in thick glasses to sweat over.

The 12 stages of the hero's journey

1. **Living in the Ordinary World:** This is the representation of the Hero's home, the safe haven to which the Special World and the journey's outcome must be compared.

   In social terms it's the shire, the village green, the town hall. In organization terms it's Brand HQ, the communal area, the hub, the place where the status quo and the current culture is most evident, the space where the brand is exemplified by "how we do things here."

   If done properly, it's what you identify at the initial stage of the brand diagnostic. If ignored, it's the neglected legacy of the business which will act as the last defensive line, the Alamo, the rallying point for employees who feel threatened and unappreciated by the enforcers of change.

   Regardless of where the line of sight of the leaders may be, for their employees the journey begins in the Ordinary World, moves to the Special World during the change, but most importantly returns to the Ordinary World once the objective is achieved. It's interesting to reflect on how many change programs are launched by virtual strangers and promise that "things will never be the same again." This promise flies in the face of the most basic storytelling principle, that the change journey is undertaken to make the Ordinary World a better place, to overcome a threat, not to transfer the people to New Worlds like so many disaffected and displaced corporate refugees.

2. **Call to Adventure:** The Call to Adventure is the catalyst moment, the initiating event that sets the story rolling by disrupting the comfort

of the Hero's Ordinary World, presenting a challenge or quest that must be undertaken. The universe is under threat or a new competitor has joined the market. In corporate speak this is usually couched in unengaging, impersonal terms such as "the change imperative," "burning platform" or, my favorite, "critical point of inflection."

3. **Refusal of the Call:** The Everyman Hero is usually reluctant to take on the journey because of fears and insecurities that have surfaced from the Call to Adventure, which may be too audacious, too intimidating or, more likely, too uninspiring. The Hero may not be willing to make changes, understandably preferring the safe haven of the Ordinary World.

   In classic corporate change terms, without support the Hero finds it hard to move through the shock, numbness and denial phases and to overcome fear. These are normal human reactions to change, usually followed by unproductive stagnation at the anger and depression stages unless appropriate measures are taken.

   If Everyman employees are to accept the need for change and to do something different as a result they certainly need to be suitably engaged and energized. The Refusal is an important stage in the journey as the Hero or champion's vulnerability encourages empathy in the audience, who can relate to the risks involved in the road that lies ahead. Without risks and danger or the likelihood of failure, the Hero's peers and colleagues will not be engaged and are unlikely to feel compelled to connect with the Hero or the journey.

   This vulnerability is often something else missing when senior Hero leaders "present" the change imperative and make the earnest call like indomitable automatons, only to scratch their heads when fewer people step into the breach than they wanted.

4. **Meeting with the Mentor:** No Hero is an island. Most brands have pasts. Most organizations have some form of legacy, often embodied by colleagues who've experienced the change journey before. At this stage in the journey, the Hero meets a Mentor to gain confidence, insight, counsel, training or magical gifts to overcome the initial fears and face the threshold of the adventure. The Mentor may be a physical person, or an object such as a map, a logbook or other writing. In organization terms think best practices, people panels and techniques like appreciative inquiry.

In corporate takeover situations, for example, it is very unwise to fail to recognize the power of the Mentor when downsizing.

5. **Crossing the Threshold:** Crossing the Threshold signifies that the Hero has finally committed to the journey. There's no going back. The champion has passed through the gateway that separates the Ordinary World from the Special World and the road of trials. It's the point of no return.

   This can be very powerfully depicted during a brand refresh engagement process, the launch of a new mission or as part of a group commitment to a change program by facilitating some form of literal totemic or symbolic rite of passage like signing up to a wall of commitment, literally stepping across a mark, dismantling a previous totem, walking through a doorway, or adding a component to a new product/design/group work of art.

6. **Tests, Allies, Enemies:** Having crossed the threshold, the Hero faces tests, encounters allies, confronts enemies, and through trial and error learns the rules of this Special World. The Hero needs to discover for himself who can be trusted. Allies are earned; a sidekick may join up, or an entire Hero team recruited.

   Brand facilitators and internal change agents co-opted onto special projects and change teams fall into this category. They are unlikely to be brand champions in the truest sense; they don't have all the answers but are early adopters volunteering to assist their peers during the transformation journey.

   The Hero must prepare himself for the greater ordeals yet to come and needs this stage to test his skills and powers, or perhaps seek further training from the Mentor. This initiation into the Special World also tests the Hero's commitment to the journey, and questions whether he can succeed.

   The current corporate predilection for short-term performance contracts and locum placements is significantly impacting relationship management and this stage in the journey in particular. If the Hero doesn't have time to establish allies the brand champion's journey promises to be a lonely and very difficult one.

7. **Approach to the Inmost Cave:** The Inmost Cave is at the journey's heart, the site of the central ordeal. During the project management and planning stages, maps may be reviewed, attacks planned,

strategies refined, a reconnaissance launched, and possibly the enemy forces whittled down before the Hero can face his greatest fear or the supreme danger lurking in the Special World. The approach may be a time for some romance or a few jokes before the battle, or it may be dominated by a ticking clock or a heightening of the stakes.

In change terms, the Inmost Cave can literally be the project planning office where change processes are configured, or behaviorally it can relate to the process of defining core behaviors to create an aspirational corporate culture. It can symbolize the planning before the psychological battle to engage employees with the values of the brand and to encourage the voluntary adoption of more effective ways of working.

8. **Ordeal**: This is the central life-or-death crisis, during which the Hero faces his greatest fear, confronts his most difficult challenge and experiences "death," the end of "normal." Within the organization this may be switchover day, when new processes first come into play; the day the redundancies take place, the old signage is torn down or the takeover actually happens; the first day of a new job when the employer brand projected in the brochures and talk meets the reality and so on.

It's what happens on the job when the phoney war of the brand launch and brand awareness workshops are over. The Hero's journey teeters on the brink of failure and his faith is tested to the full. The ordeal is the central magical stage of the journey. In corporate culture terms this is the moment when the key players have to face up to the shortcomings of the current culture, replace redundant behaviors and start to refreeze the new. Only through "death" or by bringing an end to the old ways can the Hero be reborn, experiencing a resurrection that grants greater power or insight to see the journey to the end.

9. **Reward**: The Hero has survived annihilation, overcome his greatest fear, slain the dragon or weathered the crisis of the heart, and now earns the reward that he has sought. In mythical terms, the Hero's reward comes in many forms: a magical sword, an elixir, greater knowledge or insights, riches, a new power, reconciliation with a lover. In organization terms it may well be the new product launch, new brand and livery, different structure, engaged employees, fresh

approach to values and behaviors, innovative ideas, a performance award or bonus.

Whatever the treasure, the Hero has earned the right to celebrate. However, in classic storytelling parlance, the Shadow Forces race to reclaim the Elixir that must not see the light of the Ordinary World. In corporate terms, old behaviors are hard to overcome, old habits inevitably bounce back and the external market will inevitably respond to the change.

10. **The Road Back**: The Hero's journey isn't one of selfishness or self-righteousness. It is only complete when he commits to the road back to the Ordinary World. A Hero's success in the Special World may make it difficult to return. Like Crossing the Threshold, the Road Back needs an event that will push the Hero back through the Threshold, back into the Ordinary World. The event should reestablish the central dramatic question, pushing the Hero to action and heightening the stakes. The Road Back is a moment when the Hero must choose between the journey of a higher cause and the personal journey of the heart.

    Brand champions are defined at this point. Having been through a process of change, supported by the organization, the organization has to work hard to create the conditions to keep its champions and ensure they are deployed in a way that sets a working example to their peers and become brand advocates in the truest sense. Investment will be lost if they don't go on to mentor the next generation of heroes. The more first line managers who are true brand champions, the more people they can influence and the stronger the brand.

11. **Resurrection**: The Hero faces the Resurrection, his most dangerous meeting with closure or death. This final life-or-death ordeal shows that the Hero has maintained and can apply all that he has brought back to the Ordinary World. This ordeal and Resurrection can represent a "cleansing" or purification that must occur now that the Hero has emerged from the land of the dead. The Hero is reborn or transformed, with the attributes of the ordinary self in addition to the lessons and insights from the characters he has met along the road.

    The Resurrection may be a physical ordeal or a final showdown between the Hero and the Shadow. This battle is for much more than the Hero's life. Other lives, or an entire world, may be at stake, and the Hero must now prove that he has achieved heroic status and willingly accept his sacrifice for the benefit of the Ordinary World.

The Hero needs to return to his functional role a transformed person and to inspire others by leading by example. He needs to permanently change practices which will no longer support the achievement of the desired goals and undertake tasks that role model "on brand" behavior.

Other allies may come to the last-minute rescue to lend assistance, but in the end the Hero must rise to the sacrifice at hand. He must deliver the blow that destroys the competition or redundant ways of working. He must lead by example and do things differently or do different things.

12. **Return with the Elixir:** The Return with the Elixir is the final reward earned on the Hero's journey. The Hero has been transformed, resurrected, purified, and has earned the right to be accepted back into the Ordinary World and to share the Elixir of the journey. The true Hero returns with an Elixir to share with others or heal a wounded land. The Elixir can be a great treasure or magic potion or a new way of working. It could be love, wisdom or simply the experience of having survived the Special World.

Even the tragic end to a Hero's journey can yield the best Elixir of all, granting the audience greater wisdom through the ultimate sacrifice. We all know role models who've left or have been the last to turn out the lights after shutting down a redundant branch or function.

The brand hero or champion's journey in summary

Everyman is inhabiting his ordinary organization role within an established brand, the ORDINARY WORLD, when they receive the CALL TO ADVENTURE to help drive change and create a culture that ensures some form of brand refresh and new way of working.

Depending on how they receive the call, they will be RELUCTANT at first, require clarification or a convincing argument, or REFUSE THE CALL in an attempt to maintain the status quo but are

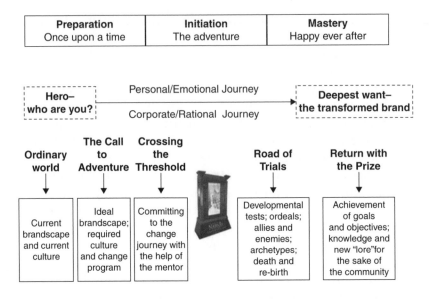

FIGURE 2   **The hero or brand champion's change journey**

encouraged by a MENTOR, a respected leader or a colleague who can help them appreciate the business case, who has experienced the journey and can help them to move out of their comfort zone and CROSS THE FIRST THRESHOLD and enter the Special World. This could be a tailored program or change initiative but it will involve engaging activity over and above what they do in the Ordinary World.

Once they have accepted the call things will never be quite the same again.

During the change process, they will encounter TESTS, ALLIES AND ENEMIES, all of which will engage their skills and test their values.

Provided they resolve these challenges, they will eventually APPROACH THE INMOST CAVE, a place where they will have to explore for themselves what change actually means and where their convictions will be tested. They will need to adapt their value set and behaviors and way of working, crossing a second threshold in the process. Here they endure the ORDEAL. The new values are put to the test.

If they succeed, they take possession of their REWARD. This could include knowledge, experience, achievement of financial or customer service related benefits or new status. But they only become a champion or hero if they return, and they are pursued on THE ROAD BACK to the Ordinary World as the cynics and competitors catch up.

They cross the third threshold, where their new ways of working must yield results by turning personal advocacy into a change movement and they then experience a RESURRECTION of enthusiasm, energy and results, and are transformed by the experience.

Finally, they RETURN WITH THE ELIXIR, a boon or treasure, to benefit the Ordinary World, whether this is hard, bottom line results, best practice stories to tell, reward and recognition or transformed brand perceptions.

Once they return, their journey will become the stuff of legend and will hopefully, with a little support from the organization itself, pass into the lore, the cache of stories of the organization and the evolution of the brand.

Pause for a second and consider where you currently are in your role and where the organization you represent is on the change journey. If your organization is considering a brand refresh, how are you going to position the need for change and the likely impact it will have on the ordinary world, the current status quo? Who will deliver the change message? What archetype role do they need to adopt to best convey the message?

Now consider the role of your change agents and the way you develop and deploy your brand ambassadors. Reflecting on Campbell's Hero's Journey model, are you truly creating engaged role models who are inspiring their peers because they can relate to them and have earned their respect? Or are you trying to shortcut the process and impose brand champions or even mercenaries on people just because the brand management team are several steps ahead in the change journey (as it's their job to be) and they are incentivized to generate brand activity?

Given the learnings we can draw from Campbell's storytelling model, is it really possible to enforce compliance and align people behind a new brand in a sustainable way? If you buy into the link between involvement and engagement and the need to engage the majority rather than conscript a minority, how are you going to do it? How can you use the values to appeal to people's storytelling instincts and rally round the brand flag?

If we accept the notion of the monomyth, the single structure underpinning most stories, and the constancy of Campbell's Hero's Journey structure then:

- it's clear that brand champions need to possess qualities that suggest they have been through an appropriate apprenticeship
- brand champions are nothing without a sense of context, the change or brand development journey
- the most effective brand heroes are those drawn from the Everyman community

So:

- champions need a real context and compelling cause
- they need to be depicted as everymen so that their exploits are achievable and representative of their community
- the title implies qualities that people instinctively know
- the change journey breaks down into phases we are hardwired by our cultural norms to understand
- champions aren't unique; they're everymen

In my view brand champions aren't the conscripted few. They are simply people who are exceptional because they willingly embark on the journey and they bring brands to life through their everyday actions. They are brand champions in the marathon of the ordinary world not just at the high-pressure sprint events at the brand conference or launch. It just so happens that the ordinary world in which they operate is the corporate rather than social community. The ordinary world of the Everyman brand champion is a source of best practice. Clearly the more Everyman brand champions there are the better.

Rather like the 1990s obsession with kaizen and TQM, the trick is not to pin the badge on a select few but to recognize that brand is mainly behavioral and to create a brand champion culture full of brand advocates which will eventually be role modeled by the majority. If you don't, then "brand," like quality management, becomes something that is hopefully done somewhere else by somebody else for everyone else.

Yes, it is helpful to enroll change agents to help facilitate the brand engagement process amongst their peers and participate in

FIGURE 3   **Two brand champions at work at British Gas**

a structured engagement program. But unless they can prove their credentials and lead by example they are more like random arche-types on the brand development journey than advocates, heroes or champions. Yes, you do want to publicize and celebrate role mod-els in an appropriate and positive manner. But the primary goal must be to create a unified culture based upon the brand values and to entice all existing and potential employees to want to join the party, to cross the threshold. The aim has to be to create an inclu-sive organization of brand advocates and not an exclusive clique of sycophants.

I disagree with commentators who view brand champions as an elite, conscripted group of brand enforcers who "do brand" to others, while their colleagues seemingly fall into the:

- brand agnostic
- brand cynic or
- brand saboteur/terrorist camps

Can any business really expect a conscripted few to cover all cus-tomer touch points?

In fact, whenever I ask the representatives from the organizations who have featured in the case studies in this book "What percentage of the organization do you consider to be brand champions?" the answer's never less than the majority of employees. The ordinary world within organizations where brand engagement abounds is one where the brand is at the core of the culture and is reflected in people processes such as performance management, induction, training, recruitment and communication.

The extent to which the term "brand champion" is acceptable in different environments has a lot, in my view, to do with the cause in question, the Call to Adventure. Being willing to champion something certainly implies that you're engaged with it. But do employees willingly engage with and champion the brands they work for but don't have an equity stake in? Alternatively, can they be conscripted to align with brands? In my experience the answer to these questions is "yes but it depends" and "yes but not for very long." Hopefully by the end of this book I'll have explained why.

THE BRAND CHAMPION AND THE BRAND MAVERICK

Champions are propelled by desire, not compelled by fear.
Denis Waitley

There's something about being a champion or ambassador on behalf of a corporate organization that's pretty "uncool." This appears to be increasingly the case in these iconoclastic and maverick times when it makes sense to be anti-establishment as so many arms of the establishment appear to have let people down, leading to government scandals, loss of faith in religious institutions, collapse in national economies, and cynicism.

It's hard to trust what our board members say these days.
A line manager at an FMCG company

If you're a defender of the meek, a Robin Hood rather than a King John, it's easy to come across as noble, self-deprecating, compassionate even. Rebels are usually attractive to those who aren't part of the establishment, especially if the prevailing status quo projects values that are self-serving and anti-social.

Consider how Virgin, sometimes overtly and other times by implication, projects itself against British Airways, for example; the Malmaison hotel chain vs. the Hilton empire; the Innocent brand vs. all other sugary drinks brands; or even Apple vs. Microsoft.

But how many brands have the luxury of being or remaining "guerrilla" brands, and if they do, how do they retain their fringe image when they are seeking mainstream income?

If you're on the side of the big battalions, if you are a champion of the so-called establishment, you're more likely to be perceived as a bully or, even worse, a dupe or a clone. Whether a David or a Goliath, either way you'll be defined by the brand on your banner regardless of whether it's made of silk or rags, whether it carries a sexy scarlet livery or the national flag.

It's hard to reconcile the two positions of maverick guerrilla and brand champion for a corporate empire. But it can be done. It's achieved largely by understanding the importance of the *willing* portion of the equation. In fact it really has to be done if any of us is to cling onto the notion that an organization, a coming together of people for mutual benefit, is going to persist as a way of driving value for us all and even enriching society. It has to be done if we're to keep the discipline needed to run an organization and reconcile it with the freedom needed to innovate and drive change. It has to be done if we're to recognize that organizations need cogs of all shapes and sizes to keep them functioning and keep them engaged and satisfied enough to help the organization stay ahead of the competition.

The secret to connecting employees with brands and vice versa, especially in these information saturated days, is being authentic and explicit rather than underhand or duplicitous about the values the brand stands for. You need to allow and enable people to make decisions about the flags they adopt themselves by providing them with the information they need to make informed choices. Fail to do so and you risk mutiny or worse.

Virgin and British Airways both attract passionate employees for very different reasons. But their loyal customers are fairly confident that the brand promise and brand reality are a close match. As an organization, whether you're looking to attract customers, investors or employees or to reassure shareholders and pressure groups, giving good brand starts with being clear about your corporate brand positioning.

BRAND ASSIMILATION: CEMEX CASE STUDY

Following European financial services giant Santander's acquisitions of Alliance and Leicester and Bradford and Bingley in 2008/09, employee engagement levels suffered, as the Santander corporate culture and the culture which underpinned the acquired brands did not initially blend well. But as Santander's HR Director, Mark Adams, nominated for HR director of the year by *HR* magazine, has famously said: *"There is only one way of doing things following a merger – but a lot of ways of dressing that up using nice words. You have to do your best to face the issues quickly because if staff don't buy in, they become terrorists"* (*HR Magazine*, June 18, 2010).

Tough words but they make the point. Adams and his team eventually managed to turn around post-merger integration and achieve double digit swings in the employee engagement statistics by leading and persisting with engaging internal communication which actively sold the benefits of merger to employees. But most importantly, they also sent key line managers on placements at Santander HQ in Madrid to see the benefits and experience the parent culture for themselves. Apparently, having addressed the culture and employee engagement issues, only now do they feel ready to re-brand their entire branch network with the parent livery.

Whatever the catalyst, from a major ownership change through to a brand refresh, the fast track to sustainable success is by creating brand advocates amongst as large a cadre of the colleague community as possible. This means developing advocates who will be willing to:

- promote the merged brand amongst colleagues, friends and family as a responsible company
- recommend the merged brand to colleagues, friends and family as a great place to work
- recommend their products and services to colleagues, friends and family
- promote the brand amongst colleagues, friends and family as a good business to deal with/invest in

Santander initiated this process via their first line managers, recognizing their highly influential nature and the need for change mentors and everyman role models who would walk the talk. Now consider the similar approach of global brand CEMEX.

Renowned for its acquisitive approach to growth, the CEMEX leadership team balances brand positioning, diversity and consistency of approach and, most importantly, delivery of the brand promise. Having made so many acquisitions, they have learned the power of brand development, about the need to clearly define the brand within the key communities and thereby use the brand as a means of sharing accountability, managing change and preserving brand equity.

I have a long-standing relationship with Tim Stokes, one of their regional VPs, which extends back to before RMC was acquired by CEMEX over five years ago. He was originally one of the executive team attempting to bolster the RMC brand in order to retain its independence. He has since flourished as a champion of both the merger and the CEMEX brand, won over by their approach to integration and brand assimilation.

Over the past century, CEMEX has grown from a local player in building materials to a leading global player in their industry. They believe they have the people, the culture, the core brand strength and the opportunities to continue on their path of disciplined growth.

Since the mid-1990s, CEMEX has expanded rapidly, both organically and through a series of strategic acquisitions in markets around the world. The result is a company comprising managers and employees from many different countries, cultures and organizations working efficiently and in a synchronized fashion across national boundaries and national cultures.

CEMEX's stated goal is to continue developing an organization in which their employees are proud and empowered to concentrate on their development and take ownership of their future. The CEMEX board recognizes the value of their brand and the fact that it is the CEMEX employees who sustain and nurture that brand as brand advocates.

Consequently, the CEMEX values include:

Collaboration: We work together and share knowledge in a collective pursuit of excellence.

Integrity: We act with honesty, responsibility, and respect toward others at all times.

Leadership: We envision the future and focus our efforts on service, excellence, and competitiveness.

It's a powerful combination stressing authenticity and working together. They work hard to role model these values at every level, especially during times of change.

Importantly, CEMEX undertook a formal brand valuation at a pivotal stage in their acquisition of RMC in the UK, feeling that it was important to quantify the value of this otherwise intangible asset. They understand and fully appreciate the importance of their brand and the business case for increasing and not diluting the value of their brand with each acquisition.

It's a learning many a mergers and acquisitions specialist should take on board, namely to give a financial value to the brands in question and protect and enhance brand equity via the colleague community, especially when looking to amalgamate the corporate cultures that underpin the merging brands.

The CEMEX board also understands how integral their employees are to achieving the growth they strive for, as Jose Antonio Gonzalez Flores, Senior VP Corporate Communications and Public Affairs, states:

Our employees are the heart of CEMEX. Our top priority is to ensure their health, safety, and well-being. We recognize the substantial intellectual and social capital that our global workforce represents, and strive to create an environment in which all of our employees can reach their full potential. We encourage innovation, collaboration, integrity, and a shared commitment to corporate responsibility.

The CEMEX leaders believe that the CEMEX brand connects emotionally with their people, building a sense of pride for the reputation of CEMEX as an admired and successful organization. It's a core philosophy that is tested time and again, especially every time they grow through acquisition.

To reinforce this belief and communicate in a continuous manner with their employees, encouraging dialog wherever possible, several channels are used:

- "Get to know CEMEX" provides information about diverse areas of the organization
- comprehensive education programs for specific career development levels (professionals in development, scholarships, CIMP, GLP) are organized to provide a holistic education to key employees and executives, cross-fertilize ideas and develop networks

- post-merger integration (PMI) facilitates the sharing of best practices between CEMEX and acquired companies, in a framework of openness and, most importantly, *mutual* respect
- day-to-day communication channels include their intranet (CEMEX Plaza), periodicals (*Our Voice*) and scheduled face-to-face briefings in offices and on site

Perhaps surprisingly they also embrace social media and have CEMEX sites on Twitter and Facebook, as well as an internal platform with social media capabilities to facilitate collaboration and innovation across the company. But they place a lot of their emphasis on face-to-face communication.

"Line managers are particularly important throughout our global network," says Tim, *"by ensuring that employee and customer touch points provide a brand experience in line with the defined brand strategy."*

It sounds a little rich in process management speak for many tastes but is appropriate for their market and their people, and with so many successful mergers and acquisitions under their banner, it's an approach that clearly works.

People processes such as recruitment, induction, communication and performance management are very closely tied to the CEMEX brand:

- an "on-boarding" orientation program provides the new joiners with a detailed story about CEMEX's history, business strategy, mission, values and code of ethic and business conduct.
- CEMEX has embedded in its organizational DNA key principles (entrepreneurship, teamwork, creativity, growth, competitiveness) that guide development and continuous improvement. These principles/ideals serve as clear reference points for the skills and competencies that are required for CEMEX employees to advance in the organization

One of the things that sets CEMEX apart is their ability to rapidly identify best practices throughout the organization and implement them. They make a point of identifying and appreciating what the unique and performance-enhancing aspects are of the organizations which join the CEMEX group and of the brands which blend into the CEMEX family, and they have a tried and tested formula for ensuring that mergers work.

Brand champions as bridge builders and role models

During the post-merger phase, rather than stripping out first line supervisors, CEMEX has a deliberate policy of flying what they consider to be their brand champions to other countries to mentor and lead the integration of new operations into CEMEX. They certainly aren't five star cheerleaders or yes men, and their role is a lot more than glorified process managers. They are selected for their people and communication skills first and foremost as their role is as much a leadership and culture-sharing function as a technical one. They are the walking embodiment of the CEMEX way but most importantly are primarily tasked with merging best practices from both organizational cultures. They don't just impose the tried and tested CEMEX processes; they look to grow and develop them in light of the new. Hands-on brand champion postings of this nature can last anything from three months to a year.

Not everyone within CEMEX can be considered a brand champion, and when an organization achieves rapid growth through acquisition it inevitably takes time to restore confidence and to allow people to get used to change. But the way CEMEX has made the link between brand equity and employee advocacy and the way they position employees as such an important part of their ongoing growth strategy is refreshing.

Given the success of their approach to embracing diversity yet developing a common culture within the company, their promotion of brand champions who have been through their own change journeys has clearly borne dividends.

The global recession has obviously done the building industry no favors, but with this inclusive, engaging approach to brand development, how long before CEMEX makes it onto the top brand table?

I like jobs that offer challenges and career opportunities, and in my opinion, I have chosen the best company to achieve my objectives. CEMEX is a very dynamic growing company.

Ildikó Papp
Cost Team Leader, Shared Service Center
CEMEX, Hungary

CEMEX encourages innovation and enables all of their people to grow in a challenging, creative work environment. People put forth their best efforts, knowing the company will support their initiatives.

Javier Merle
Sustainable Development Director
CEMEX, Spain

CEMEX offers a very professional and dynamic atmosphere, where values and ethics are extremely important. Working at CEMEX is a never-ending learning process.

Kamla Sherif Nassar
Human Resource Projects & Information Manager
CEMEX, Egypt

TOP CASE STUDY TIPS:

- Recognize the power of colleagues as brand advocates and use brand champions, especially line managers, to lead the post-merger brand integration process as walking role models and mentors but also as facilitators of two-way best practice sharing.
- Respect the Ordinary World of both parties when communicating before, during and after major change.
- Use existing champions to position change as another phase in the narrative surrounding an ongoing journey.

PART 2

WHAT'S EMPLOYEE ENGAGEMENT?

I had the rare pleasure of diving near a beautiful reef off Key West several years ago, when the tranquility was shattered by the sudden arrival of a large boat containing around 50 snorkeling day trippers. In an instant the fish scattered, the water became a frothing mass of fins, bubbles and elbows, the air was alive with excited chattering in a dozen languages and the water literally clouded over. Something similar has happened to the employee engagement space in the past decade or so.

As often happens when a topic attracts enthusiasm, passion and energy, our senses are overloaded and we lose sight of what is essentially a relatively simple concept. To clarify my own take on this subject, I define the increasingly obscured term "brand engagement" as the sense of willing connection between stakeholders and brands based on values and resulting in increased loyalty and improved performance. It is dependent upon free will and requires an emotional as well as a rational connection.

Employee or internal brand engagement is a means to an end not an end in itself. It represents the most mature or advanced form of internal communication at the opposite end to the push mode of communication. It is not something different from internal communication, as some critics imply, because employee engagement and communication are inextricably linked. Brand engagement in the internal market is simply the process of clarifying and forging a relationship between employees and the brand they represent in a way that ensures they are able to deliver on the promise the brand makes to the market, the place where the value the organization adds is judged, whatever that market may be.

An organization's brand is the physical and behavioral identity it presents to all stakeholders, the four C's, not just customers. This means that brands are as relevant to employees within the not-for-profit and public sector as they are in the commercial sector as drivers of engagement, culture development and performance.

As lasting engagement is based on free will, the implication is that engagement is conditional on authenticity. Absolutely. Whether they physically leave or not, people don't tend to stick around when they don't trust what the business is saying; and for the business read first line manager and then all other forms of corporate communication, in that order. Lasting engagement, in my view, is entirely conditional on authenticity because, as the saying goes, "You can fool some of the people some of the time but you can't fool all of the people all of the time."

Engagement is more emotional than rational, and unless someone bothers to measure it we tend to take it for granted. At least until the relationship breaks down, resulting in extreme cases in brand sabotage and/or industrial action.

Employee engagement isn't a nice-to-have which is only relevant in the good times. There's a very clear and long-established business case for it. Consider this sample of metrics favoring the brand engagement cause.

Market research leader Gallup asserts that, in 2008, the cost of disengagement to the UK economy was between £59bn and £64bn, and an IES/Work Foundation report found that, if organizations increased investment in engagement practices by just 10%, they would increase profits by up to £2k per employee per year (*Employee Engagement Today*, vol. 2, Autumn 2009).

As someone who has first-hand experience of the impact disaffected staff can have on business performance and brand management, I believe these to be conservative figures, but they still make a very strong point.

David Bolchover, in his book *The Living Dead*, states that in the UK alone, doctors receive over 9mn "suspect" requests for sick notes per year. This is equivalent to the entire population of Sweden.

In addition, one in three midweek visitors to a major theme park is reputedly "pulling a sickie" from work. Great news for the entertainment industry but worrying for HR departments. It also begs the question where do the theme park employees go when they fancy a duvet day?

A 2006 study by ISR found that a 5% improvement in the overall level of employee engagement converts into a 25%–85% increase in profits for service oriented organizations.

Jack Welch, legendary former CEO of GE, identified employee engagement as the most important barometer of organizational performance ("A Healthy Company," *Business Week*, May 3, 2006).

The CBI reports that apparent sickness absence costs the UK economy more than £13bn a year. Business case for employee engagement at an individual business level aside, recovery of that figure would go a long way toward solving the national debt problem.

Measurement specialists PeopleMetrics, in a 2007 White Paper "So Employee Engagement Matters...What Next?," have gone so far as to suggest that we should stop asking *why*, take it as read and focus exclusively on *how*. I agree with them.

Of course, employee engagement isn't necessarily dependent upon an overt reference to the brand. But it makes a lot of sense to link the two. In fact many aspects of corporate life can be engaging in the wider sense. From the temporary feel-good stemming from a one-off event through to waiting with sweaty palms with your colleagues to hear who's being "resized," being engaged with something isn't necessarily synonymous with having a good time for a long time. It is possible to be engaged with negative events or cynicism (consider the power of the unofficial underground resistance movement when employees rebel quietly against the status quo).

But overtly leveraging the brand can and should be the keystone of positive employee engagement given the intimate if often misunderstood relationship between the brand and the culture or way things are done within the organization. Overt focus on the brand isn't the only factor driving employee engagement but it's an increasingly important factor. And employee engagement is most definitely essential for effective, holistic brand management.

The success of a brand isn't entirely down to the marketing department, despite corporate game playing that suggests otherwise. Marketing specialists, after all, simply make the promises. Whether they like it or not they rely on employees to keep them.

As organizations like CEMEX who've placed a numerical value on their brand appreciate, failure to engage employees with the brand or connect the internal world of the organization to the external positioning of the organization is tantamount to slow brand suicide.

Brands need to be managed from within as diligently and passionately as they are promoted beyond the corporate borders.

Enlightened employees, however, can't be managed in the same way as the physical brand assets. They can't really be conscripted to become brand champions nor can they be aligned with the brand like just another tied supplier. This is largely because to all intents and purposes they *are* the brand. Most employees see themselves as existing in the first person *"I am the brand when I interact with others"* (UK call center operative). Treat them in the third person and lecture them about the brand at your peril.

EMPLOYEE ENGAGEMENT'S ALL TALK

Certainly since *Brand Engagement* was published, much has been written about the concept of employee engagement as this relatively modern phenomenon continues to evolve from its internal communication roots. Just look at the networking site LinkedIn and search for internal communication or employee engagement and you'll stumble across dozens of dedicated trans-global communities all exchanging perspectives on the subject and tactical hints and tips. The wider information superhighway is abuzz with sites like The Employee Engagement Forum dedicating a great deal of bandwidth to what was once a seemingly simple concept, and professional bodies like the CIPR have established dedicated employee engagement subgroups to cater to this growing market.

I maintain my stance that, however entertaining and useful, applications like Facebook will never replace Facetime. But I entirely agree with Tom Peters that with regard to employee engagement, there's a little too much "talking" and worryingly little "doing" for my taste.

Whatever the resources available or however crowded the airwaves, employees don't need more definitions; they need action. The recent crash in world markets illustrates why.

Consider the financial services industry. Despite all the talk about regulation and the size of the financial services supertankers which seemingly foundered on the jagged rocks of gambling and greed, at the heart of the banking crisis was the fact that they were operating beyond the remit of their core values. Quite simply, they were projecting one brand image, usually based on trust, customer focus and ethics, but delivering another.

In what is essentially a service industry, sustainable relationship management was coming a distant second to short-term profiteering and over-reliance on complexity and customer inertia. Employee and wider stakeholder engagement was undermined as a result to the point that arguably virtually an entire sector became morally and then literally bankrupt.

FINANCIAL SERVICES BRANDS RUNNING ON EMPTY – A TEN-STEP REFUELING PLAN

During the run-up to the recent UK election, like many people, I watched the public debating forums and was shocked by the apparent paucity of basic knowledge amongst pundits and public alike about the key issues which recently sent world financial markets and economies into a tailspin. The same observation applies to the debate in other important global economies like the US, France and Germany.

Most pundits blame the regulators and national governments. But the current recession has very little to do with regulation. It has predominantly been caused by the brand schizophrenia conveyed by much of the financial services sector which has caused stakeholders both within and beyond the corporate HQ to disengage with the leading brands. It hasn't happened overnight and wasn't caused by a single deal or isolated company.

That's a fairly punchy statement, so let me deconstruct it. Many of the premier, informed critics and commentators of the sector, typified by Will Hutton, who has been a leading writer on matters financial for over thirty years, and Richard Edelman (of Edelman Trust Barometer fame), point to a fundamental breakdown in trust between:

- the institutions and *customers*
- the institutions and *shareholders*
- the institutions and other *institutions*

But in my view the worst breakdown has been between the institutions and *their employees*.

Governments rather belatedly appear to have "rumbled" the core structural cause of the meltdown of the sector, namely the convenient blending of the high-risk investment banking operations with the steady cash cow of retail operations. It's going to be tough disentangling them. But even as the structural wrecking crews belatedly move in, the critics are missing a more insidious issue. Deep-seated culture management issues are at the absolute core of the financial services brand management problem and reputation can't be recovered overnight.

The media, in the main, has targeted the once heroic and now infamous senior leaders. But if we allow ourselves to obsess about hunting tabloid scapegoat caricatures of "Fred the Shred" and his peer group we're in grave danger of very much missing the point. The shortcomings of the directors/lapsed hero leaders themselves and the problems the financial districts face are merely the symptoms of a much more invidious infection – the notion of the so-called performance culture tied into quarterly stock market reporting.

Not so long ago finance was a relationship business. Customers expected to retain a relationship with their manager for many years. Staff expected to remain loyal to one brand for most if not all of their careers and relied on fostering internal relationships and networks. In the corporate sphere, commerce conducted business to business was largely relationship based.

Even investors, including pension fund managers, had a stable relationship with banking stocks, the steady and guaranteed incremental performers which underpinned pension and investment funds. This enabled banking executives to plan and strategize for the long to medium term.

These relationship patterns and strategic approaches all changed after Big Bang.

But as the financial institutions evolved rapidly in many respects to reflect the increasing demands of investors, the march of process automation, cost-saving outsourcing and offshoring and what I believe to be the misinterpretation of the performance culture concept caused cultural schizophrenia.

The core problem is that the brands failed to evolve to reflect their operational reality. They still promised brand values like *listening*, *integrity* and *stability* to staff and customers yet were acting very differently both in the markets and arguably more importantly within. The relationships between their customers and employees became largely disingenuous.

Employees who were accustomed to five-year strategies and three-year plans became tied into the life cycle of executives in the hot seat with 18-month bouts of tenure. They were encouraged to take risks, as we're now witnessing as governments and the regulators like the Office of Fair Trading and FSA (in the UK) belatedly show their teeth, keeping the lawyers busy in the process.

Notions of customer service were subverted by apparent exploitation of customer inertia. HR had nearly all of its developmental edge undermined by process redesign. Six-monthly, key performance indicator dominated performance contracts replaced annual reviews, and increasingly locum and short-term contracts began to phase out loyalty bonuses and expensive benefits packages.

None of these factors would be sufficient on its own to unilaterally bring about a catastrophe of such scale. But together these elements have slowly poisoned the well of goodwill, often through internal communication that is essentially duplicitous at source. Increasingly the words and figures failed to add up for staff and customers alike, summed up in increasing spin like the ABBEY re-brand, which, let's face it, was never going to turn banking on its head, or the proliferation of essentially insubstantial customer charters (seldom an encouraging sign).

Now, even the hitherto untouchable Masters of the Universe like Lehman Brothers have seen their brands implode, and mighty brands like the arguably untouchable Goldman Sachs are witnessing unprecedented levels of market criticism and scandal.

When the premier brands are tarnished, the financial services sector really is running on empty.

So what's to be done?

This is a case where the "hair of the dog that bit you" isn't going to put things right, but a brand refresh based around these steps just may:

1. Leadership teams should take a back to basics approach to stakeholder engagement and ensure that the *story of the evolution* of their vision, mission and strategy and brand development approach are all in harmony
2. The link between *culture and brand* needs to be recognized and so-called EVP/employer and commercial brand brought sharply back into single focus

3. A *brand valuation* should be prioritized and current and requisite *culture analysis* undertaken to start to develop a future organization culture that is fit for purpose
4. *Brand coalitions* need to be created consisting of at least Marketing/ HR and the CEO's office to ensure that the brand promised is the brand employees are able and willing to deliver
5. *Internal communication* needs to be professionalized and encouraged to shift from push communication, technical gimmicks and director-led Town Halls to encourage more intimate, local, face-to-face, two-way engagement
6. *Measurement:* The annual employee survey should be discontinued and replaced with regular, consistent pulse takes and a suite of measurement tied into a balanced scorecard for which all leaders are accountable
7. *Performance management* has to refocus on accountability over the medium term rather than encouraging short-term "win at all costs"
8. *Training and development* and *organization development* strategies must embrace the values and behaviors stemming from the brand rather than reinventing them
9. *Line managers* and first line supervisors are undoubtedly the modern pivots around which the organizations and their brand revolve. They should be recognized as such and development support provided accordingly
10. The FS organizations need to take a long and hard look at the "establishment" consultancy and *professional services supertankers* who have been advising them about how to put right problems which they played a large part in creating. Are they flexible, fleet of foot and even impartial enough to help facilitate the engagement levels to bring about the necessary change?

The hitherto unfashionable mutual societies may actually be leading the way with their values based management approaches, and word on the street is that even some of the investment banks are attempting to simplify and synchronize their organization development, brand development and communication functions.

But when you consider the adverse impact that the global financial services brand meltdown has had on world economies, it's a worrying time. As profits bounce back, will the fresh finances fuel much-needed investment in the brand infrastructure and investment in managing the organization culture that underpins brand? Or will the budgets again be spent on livery enhancements and advertising to entice customers and investors back through the doors, lured by false rhetoric about a performance culture that is ultimately unsustainable? Unfortunately I very much fear the latter.

Leaders within FS brands clearly need to create the space and environment in which their brand heroes can excel. But will they?

Rather than criticizing them as "nice to have" initiatives, in these tough times, brand related organization development programs should be prioritized as part of the recovery process and OD professionals should be leading the revolutionary line.

Employees and customers are craving a return to the familiarity and stability of the ordinary world. But they also need the reassurance of knowing that their leaders have learned some valuable lessons. The time has come for comprehensive internal reviews followed by an energetic repositioning of the vision, mission and values and associated people processes within many of the leading FS brand names. This should be the first step toward a reframing of the definition of performance in the context of the employer or employment brand. But I wonder how many are conducting reviews of this nature, and if they are, do they include HR and Marketing in the same meetings? If so, is the relationship on an equal footing, or does the HR representative actually play the role of the "Bez" in the band.[1]

The notion of a performance culture is complex. But consider for a second the long-established theory that individuals are at their most effective within a role some 2.5 years into the job. Or reflect on the equally established best practice that leaders should spend most of their first 100 days listening and gathering information. Contrast this with the notion of "hitting the ground running" and the obsession with quarterly shareholder reporting, performance contracts, absence of induction/on-boarding, and year-on-year incremental targeting regardless of conditions. Mixed messages?

It seems a little old-fashioned in these high-octane times but there's sound logic underpinning leadership best practices which call for considered, well-paced decision-making based upon an understanding

---

1 Alludes to a legendary member of the indie group The Happy Mondays, renowned for having no musical talent but for entertaining the crowds with his eccentric dancing on stage.

that the decision-makers will still be around when the impact of their decisions come to fruition. How many brand champions are hit-and-run heroes?

Bankers, for example, used to be remunerated on the basis of loyalty bonuses and benefits packages at preferential rates. Not so long ago, any posting on a CV revealing tenure in a role of under three years was viewed with suspicion. Lift the drains on the recent recruitment drive amongst the retail banking sector, however, and you will be greeted by whole teams made up of job-hopping former investment bankers.

Of course the flipside of low employee turnover includes problems with innovation, pace and inertia. But inertia and stability are two very different things. The latter was once a highly prized commodity even in important parts of the investment market but was derided by the "short termists." What wouldn't shareholders and portfolio managers, for that matter, now give for even incremental returns on their investments?

Those in the know suggest that many of the high-profile leaders who will be appearing in committees over the next few years have been off-the-record advocates of culling gray hair in their staff ranks. But what price brand wisdom now?

Don't get me wrong. I very much believe in the notion of a culture of performance. That's why we're all in business after all. I just don't believe in the notion of winning at all costs. When the needs of one stakeholder community (like shareholders) undermine the satisfaction of another (like colleagues or even society at large), sustainability will suffer. I'm realistic enough to understand that sustainability, network building and relationship development are the bedfellows of integrity, accountability, security and trust (the values, ironically, most popularly used to advertise the wares of financial services brands).

I'm certainly not calling for a complete return to the old hierarchies and command and control regimes but it's clear that there's going to have to be a more substantial dose of mature, "back to the future" thinking if the nirvana of an appropriate and authentic performance culture is ever going to be achieved by arguably our most influential businesses and brands.

FS brands were, and to a great extent still are, highlighting one set of values: *trust, security, solidity* and promising relationship management, while delivering another set: *deceit, risk, short termism, profiting from inertia* and winning at all costs.

The outcome has been unprecedented financial crisis and loss of confidence in the brand names of an entire sector, with very worrying aftershocks undermining brands across sectors. These are tough times for frontline brand champions within the banking sector.

It's controversial to suggest so but arguably the biggest issue hasn't been regulation; if you accept that responsibility for the brand extends to HR as well as Marketing, recent brand disasters are down to chronic brand mis-management. Brand managers across sectors need to learn the lessons from their banking colleagues.

The future's not entirely doom and gloom for the sector. Performance figures seem to suggest that financial services firms bounce back relatively quickly. But do their brands? There are some leading lights, including brands like HSBC (37 in Interbrand's Top 100) and First Direct in the UK, which was remarkably ahead of its time, and innovators like Virgin and Tesco who are influencing the sector from within.

But with stakeholder trust at record low levels, they're sadly few and far between.

IS TRUST DEAD?

I was recently at a dinner party thrown by a former HR Director friend and as I arrived at his house I was first struck by the number of high-performance cars on the driveway and then, once I was introduced to his guests, was equally surprised by the fact that most were from the HR community.

I'm not deriding folk for their success. It just took a little getting used to, especially as most of the conversation revolved around the financial *benefits* associated with acquiring a reputation as a downsizing expert and "being the last one to turn out the lights" before moving on. QED – high-performance cars = redundancy packages.

It's clearly wrong to claim that resizing has become the raison d'être of the modern HRD. But my perception wasn't improved by the dinner conversation about what it really means to trust and whether trust has *any* function in the modern workplace.

One premise was that despite the fact that employees' trust in their organizations fell dramatically and steadily from 2008, organizations still need to work out new ways of reengaging and reestablishing the psychological contract with their people.

The opposite and very much prevailing view was that certain things in business will always have to remain secret, being open and honest is impossible, and people should be mature enough to accept that.

The biggest problem I have with this perspective is that secrecy is contagious. It encourages disingenuousness, and paranoia can quickly become part of the fabric of the organization, at the core of the culture. It prevents people from being themselves in the workplace and that is a proven barrier to engagement and optimum performance. I couldn't help but detect that this assembly at least relished the power associated with the latter position and I voiced disappointment that there was virtually no conversation about the positive, proactive and creative aspects of the organization and brand development responsibilities of the HR role.

Trust implies intimacy. It was interpreted by my fellow diners as *"exposing yourself to someone at your most vulnerable in the hope that they will not abuse you."* Trust has a blind quality in this context and suggests an imbalance of power. Perhaps it's time to reclaim and redefine what trust means.

The surprising consensus amongst this group of senior HR professionals was that trust has no real place at work any longer and that a healthy skepticism should prevail recognizing that the employer/employee relationship is simply "a marriage of convenience." Neutrality was preferable.

It was strongly implied that any other stance was over-emotional, even naïve. But is it possible or desirable to remain neutral in a vocational environment you devote the largest portion of your life to? Is it really possible to be neutral and engaged simultaneously? Is it possible to be neutral and be yourself or perform at your best? Can employees be neutral and engaged, neutral and truly satisfied?

This discussion was speaking volumes about the root cause of employee disengagement with their organization and by implication, the brand as positioned by the internal marketing usually stemming from HR.

The HR community has been banging on about employee engagement for some time now. Engagement requires an emotional connection. Trust is a fairly fundamental emotion. If there's no trust there's no psychological contract between employees and the employer. Without that there's no "extra mile" and no relationship development. Has this airtime really just been internal PR and spin?

I appreciate that most HRDs I seem to meet these days are vassals of the process reengineers, edged out by SAP and similar apparent technological breakthroughs in people process management, and have become de-sensitized to emotions in a similar way to soldiers on the frontline. But is this a reflection of behavior born of survival or how they really believe things should be?

The Demming lovers will have us believe that organizations are essentially 80%+ process and little else; that people are drivers of "nonconformance" and so on. So where does all the creativity and emotion go when people hang up their coats at corporate HQ?

Are we giving up on values like loyalty, decency, fairness, ethical behavior, empathy and so on, which all rely on trust to function? And what are customers to think of bold brand promises made by organizations in which trust is consigned to the naïve and the vulnerable?

I guess you can have a relationship or marriage of convenience based on neutrality, without passion, empathy and drive. But then you can also truss yourself up in a corset and join a Victorian role-playing society.

Trust is fundamental to sustainable employee engagement and brands can't be sustained without engaged employees. There's a lot of noise surrounding the Edelman Trust Barometer for a reason.

THE LINK BETWEEN EMPLOYEE AND BRAND ENGAGEMENT

An organization can only "walk the talk" when its managers deliberately shape its internal reality to align with its brand promise...[the brand's] values must be internalized by the organization, shaping its instinctive attitudes, behaviours, priorities, etc.

Alan Mitchell, "Out of the Shadows"
Journal of Marketing Management 15, No. 1–3,
January–April 1999: pp. 25–42

Arguably the most powerful manifestation of the organization, certainly from the customer perspective, is the brand. As I illustrate in *Brand Engagement,* employee engagement, although often overcomplicated, is no more complex than a higher-order or evolved form of internal communication.

Employee engagement with the brand, however, can't be confined to the bottom steps of the engagement staircase (see Figure 4 below) as it so often is. *"As much as some of our Internal Communication managers try to force the message home, those pesky people who work on the front line keep interpreting things for themselves,"* exclaimed a frustrated executive recently, with a deliberate tone of irony which spoke volumes. Employees have a much more intimate relationship with the brand than marketers usually give them credit for.

As Nicholas Ind states in *Living the Brand* "... *it is only the visual presentation (of brand) that is truly policeable. Content is not. Even in the tightest structures you cannot create an Orwellian world where every employee thinks and talks in the same way....The power of a brand lies in giving employees the freedom to use their imaginations within the constraints set by the organization's values*" (p. 17).

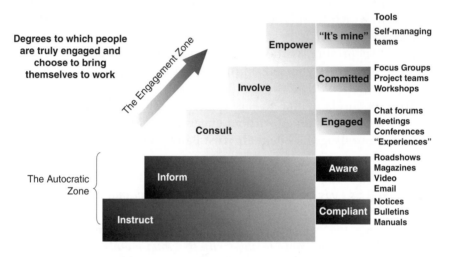

FIGURE 4   **The BY2W engagement staircase**

I prefer to think of the values as liberators of choice, bringing freedom rather than constraints. They enable employer and stakeholder communities alike to make informed choices which will directly impact the productivity of their relationship with the brand. It's clear to me that the much maligned values are clear milestones on the path to employee brand engagement.

Engagement, however, as I've said, is a means to an end, that is, more effective performance, not an end in itself. Critical to the achievement of that end is creating a culture in which people willingly go the extra mile for the brand and consistently initiate and deliver activity which is on-brand and on-objective, without being cajoled into doing so. This is especially true in these days of liberated mass media loosely termed the knowledge economy.

In the knowledge economy everyone is a volunteer, but we have trained our managers to manage conscripts.

Peter. F. Drucker

According to Human Synergistics International in their book *In Great Company*, culture change in support of brand development is vital, but it can often take three years plus. Pretty daunting if you're a board member accountable to shareholders every six months. Given the right conditions, however, and starting with a committed CEO and top team, I've certainly witnessed cultural transformation in as little as 18 months.

Australian company Adshel, one of many case studies highlighted in *In Great Company*, is a case in point. Adshel is one of the most profitable companies in the Clear Channel and APN group and, following a major culture development program, now consistently outperforms the market. Having played her part in transforming the performance of the brand by concentrating on culture change and employee engagement, Anna Lee, who, notably, is Adshel's CFO, points to a united approach taken by their key communicators which led to a shift in staff attitude toward the company. *"We now have a collective culture with real pride and passion for the Adshel brand."*

Key outcomes include:

- clear and unambiguous employee role profiles
- greatly improved internal communication and focus on communication
- skills development leading to measured improvements in employee engagement
- greater employee involvement resulting in a greater sense of empowerment, engagement and ownership
- enhanced training and development creating a sense that the company cares about its employee's higher-order needs

The general premise of employee engagement is that individual contributions of employees in the workplace are influenced by the strength of their emotional connection to and active involvement with their employer. And despite all the talk about employer, employee or employment brand, the organization for me is synonymous with the brand.

There's little point in defining a completely different brand position and value set for the external and internal audiences. Less is more, and the greater the synergy between sets of values the better. It's disingenuous at best and counterproductive and confusing at worst to pretend that the brand the customer engages with is or should be any different from the brand "presented" to employees.

Yet this confusing, "replicant" approach of creating doppelganger values sets is more common than we might think. The notion of the employer brand and employee value proposition or EVP (or more accurately the employment brand if you subtract employee experience from the internal brand promise) has rightfully gained a permanent place in corporate parlance. But every effort should be made to ensure that there is a great deal of consistency between external and internal representations of the brand. Better still, swallow your pride and opt for one brand positioning for both markets and a short list of just three powerful values (see *Brand Engagement* for discussion on the Power of Three).

The simpler, stronger, more consistent and more positive the connection between employee and brand, the more likely it is that employees will contribute their best efforts. I've yet to see an internal brand awareness campaign succeed on the basis of creating a longer list of values, subdividing the brand into customer-facing and employee-facing brand or introducing a brand personality while ignoring the core values. The simpler and more effective the connection between employee, vision, values, behaviors, competencies and brand, the more likely it is that brand champions will naturally emerge and thrive throughout the organization, largely because they will have a more connected view of the organization.

Under these conditions it doesn't take a conscripted army of superheroes to bring brands to life. This is an essential truth borne out in practice time and time again, regardless of sector and irrespective of the nature of the change imperatives affecting the organizations in question.

Consider the highly regarded Pret A Manger brand. Pret A Manger has come a long way and in less than 20 years of trading it has changed the way city workers lunch forever. In the recent past, if inner city workers wanted a snack or sandwich lunch they could go either to a specialist, independently run sandwich shop or to a supermarket where standards still vary from good to (more frequently) very bad.

Julian Metcalfe and Sinclair Beecham stepped in to fill the gap. From modest roots which were "on message" with their time, a challenger brand has rapidly grown.

The Pret Marketing department clearly has a challenge to continue to drive home the message that Pret employees make their food in each shop's kitchen every morning. They also need to communicate the nutritional value of their products. Yes, they do this at point of sale, but, products aside, the greatest asset is the demeanor, enthusiasm, consistency and energy of their brand champions, their staff, and this is clear as soon as you set foot in one of their outlets.

As Andrew Rolfe, Chairman and former Pepsico exec, points out:

We are passionate about people and our staff. They are extremely important and we make sure they have the right opportunities and rewards, that they are paid correctly and that they have fun working for us. We have and will always have a great culture and energy.

Potential colleagues are carefully screened before they join the company. Rolfe believes that sharing the company's values, which revolve around passion for products, people and the business, is essential to wanting to work for Pret.

There is a rigorous assessment for each potential employee. We make them work in a shop for a few days, they have several interviews and, in each case, we try to get to know them as individuals.

Pret staff work very hard but clearly thrive on a dynamic culture, peer-centric environment, friendly people, empowerment (they have a say in selecting their team colleagues and key decisions) and fantastic food.

For what is essentially a fast turnover food retailing business Pret's values based training and development process is very good. Pret prides itself on looking after its staff and developing them and, despite the fact it appears to have fallen out of fashion, isn't shy about using the "career" word. Surprisingly, they have a Pret Academy that handles all core training and development for the company and have been short-listed for an HR Excellence award for their talent management strategy.

Pret employees are offered special deals at many companies in a number of sectors. They also get a free breakfast and lunch every day, and generous discounts in all Pret shops.

Each employee has their lunch delivered in a named bag every day, including back-office staff. They celebrate each other's birthdays, and get together every Tuesday morning for coffee and croissants to talk about the previous week's trading and brainstorm new approaches. They are truly involved in the business of managing the brand.

Every one of the employees, including the directors, goes "back to the floor" several times a year to make sandwiches. The company donates its unsold food to charity each day. They also work on sustainability projects to reduce their environmental impact.

As a result of this cocktail of initiatives engagement levels are high. Despite the recent stake McDonald's has taken in the business, it's interesting to note that these uber food retailing process giants have not attempted to interfere with operations or "gild the lily."

The key learning from an organization like Pret A Manger is that they work hard to create an internal brand champion culture that may be pressurized but is energizing. Employees feel valued, and a lot of this is to do with the little things which they identify as a result of empowering consultation and ensuring that the leadership stays close to day-to-day working reality.

- Pret A Manger has 3889 UK employees
- Pret's UK ad spend is only 0.4% of sales
- McDonald's now has a substantial shareholding (helping the Pret brand to expand internationally)

Yes, the product, business model and processes need to be spot on. But it's the values, the people and focus on all stakeholder communities simultaneously that make the big difference, that create the brand. To date I've seen major petrochemical companies quickly recover employee and investor confidence in their brand through reengineering the way their leaders engage with employees by personalizing the brand and the values through the stories they tell. I've witnessed financial services firms achieve cultural breakthroughs by focusing on their brand values to rapidly transform their recruitment strategies. I've also seen retail firms prevent strike action from undermining their brand positioning by realizing that their staff *are* their brand and rethinking the way they connect with their employees. In each case, however, it took some sort of brand disaster to make them appreciate the power of the brand and the need to create a brand champion culture. Just think what they could have avoided and achieved had the proverbial penny dropped earlier.

Consistent levels of employee engagement can be achieved relatively quickly if:

- engagement programs role model the brand values
- engagement initiatives allow employees the freedom to experiment and explore
- internal communication functions keep things simple, connected and authentic
- measurement role models the brand values
- people processes like performance management reinforce the values

At its core, employee engagement is based upon reciprocity, the practice of exchanging things with others for mutual benefit. It involves give-and-take and implies a state where the organization and its employees exist in a condition of mutual understanding, striving for symbiosis. It isn't all about free love and flowers. It just makes very good business sense.

The implication is that the employer strives to create a work environment that is satisfying and rewarding for employees and stimulates their emotions and innate desire to address their higher-order needs. The employer literally invites them to bring themselves to work and become similarly invested (engaged) in the long-term success of their organization or brand. The premise is based on a basic understanding that:

- the organization really does recognize that employees are its greatest asset and not just the largest cost to be managed
- people innately want to be the best they can be and really do want to make the most of their time (and work is, sadly, where most people spend most of their time)
- businesses bother to "measure what they treasure" and, if they don't formally measure brand equity, invest at least some time and budget analyzing the link between advocacy and customer satisfaction

The concept of employee engagement leading to brand development is fairly simple to grasp. It's also fairly simple to understand the business case based upon some straightforward return on investment metrics compared with the cost of not bothering. But it's apparently not that easy to implement or we would be seeing a lot more hand holding between marketing and HR departments.

Interestingly, in a very recent online poll of professional communicators on the LinkedIn network, the question was posed "What is the most important role of employee communications?" Respondents answered as follows:

- 6% – getting information to people
- 8% – engaging people with change
- 12% – supporting the customer experience
- 28% – engaging people in their job
- 46% – aligning people with the strategy, vision and values

I know the internal communication market very well. I've set up IC functions and have spent the past decade pursuing the engagement agenda. I suggest that, on average, at least half of an internal communicator's time is spent pushing messages and most of the rest is spent attempting to align employees in some way behind change or strategic initiatives. Does this make the IC profession a clan of failed idealists practicing one thing yet preaching another?

Should we accept that anything other than a push communication approach is "whistling into the wind"?

Will internal communication functions ever become more than message managers?

Is the management of the brand worth adopting as part of a business transformation strategy when in surveys like this one very few people believe the role of internal communication is to support the customer experience of the brand?

Well, I hold fast to the perspective that brand equity is becoming increasingly important for both the internal and external facing parts of the business. It's a belief that has been reinforced by the demise of businesses which haven't taken brand management seriously enough to invest in employee engagement and culture development and the robustness of those who, like the Interbrand Top 100 and those featured here, have and still do.

Organizations are complex, interesting and challenging entities in their own right. One of the challenges to successful employee engagement is that emotional connections can be difficult to define and measure. They are prone to shift in response to changes in the work environment. But that's no excuse not to try. It's this very unpredictability that makes leadership fun. More confounding, however, is that these relations are influenced by multiple variables, including:

- line management relationships
- the state of internal communication
- organizational mission, vision, culture and values
- workload
- leadership
- the role of HR
- the state of people processes
- the relationship between HR and Marketing
- whether and how you measure

Get the blend right, however, and any investment pays for itself. Whatever the mix or circumstances, you can tell instantly when employees are engaged...or not, as soon as you take a call or walk up to the front desk.

Challenges aside, engagement as a strategy is not only important but also vital – especially in a climate of economic uncertainty – to the long-term viability of brands, especially when employees have rapid access to multiple communication channels and information sources.

Regardless of external forces, employee engagement can't be reserved as a "nice to do" strategy for the good times. Employees are smart and quickly spot insincerity. Whether you care about the so-called war for talent or not, existing employees and recruits alike increasingly resist internal PR and foie gras methods of force-feeding messages based on the traditional sales funnel.

Certainly for internal audiences, the persistent "funnel" approach generates activity for the internal comms department but it just doesn't work very well. I have many, but consider just one example.

A legal firm was struggling to achieve anything like the levels of understanding it needed to comply with consultation regulation and make some relatively simple changes to its final salary pension scheme. The HR department was being driven mad by the level and nature of queries which resulted from a piece of internal communication written by the Marketing team (who were responsible for what little internal communication took place). Following record levels of confusion which followed hard on the heels of a 20-page document about the changes, HR commissioned an external consultant

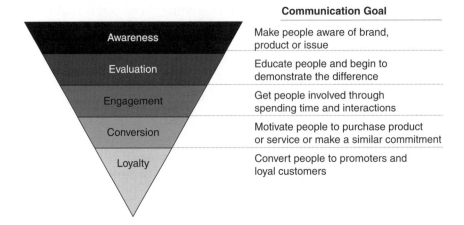

	Communication Goal
Awareness	Make people aware of brand, product or issue
Evaluation	Educate people and begin to demonstrate the difference
Engagement	Get people involved through spending time and interactions
Conversion	Motivate people to purchase product or service or make a similar commitment
Loyalty	Convert people to promoters and loyal customers

FIGURE 5   **The generic traditional sales funnel model**

to sort out the issue. The consultant, quite simply and quickly, pulled together a cross-sectional team of staff, which included senior managers and secretaries alike. She fast recognized that the most widely read piece of internal literature was a lighthearted newsletter published by the IT department which lampooned the stuffy internal culture and the attempts of the partners to "consolidate their position as a leading legal brand."

It didn't take long to collaborate and effectively rewrite the previous pension materials in terminology which didn't need barristers to interpret and to back this up with one team-briefing session.

Employee action regarding the proposed changes shifted from 16% to 73% within two weeks. A heroic effort. The firm has also employed the consultant on a full-time basis tasked with setting up a professional communication function. They are also rethinking what they mean when they talk about their brand and have rediscovered the work they did some years ago on core values.

The irony is that the rebel publication which gave the consultant her eureka moment was the subject of a great deal of partner-level unrest as many believed that, should it get into the wrong hands, it would affect their professional standing (in effect their brand).

The emphasis internally, regardless of sector, needs to be firmly placed on the engagement, experimentation and involvement stages of the communication flow process, providing plenty of opportunity

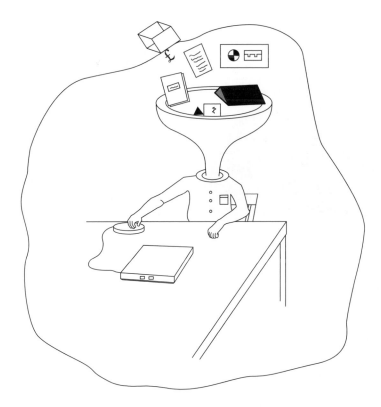

FIGURE 6   **The obviously flawed foie gras approach to internal communications**

for employees to explore and cross-check messages with their understanding of brand reality. I mentioned earlier that it's my belief that most people don't really grow up but rather learn the rules about behaving in public, which probably explains why opportunities to be liberated by the chance to play are usually greeted so enthusiastically within an otherwise stuffy corporate context. For internal audiences the appropriate approach to communication is a complete inversion of the external sales funnel.

Of course employees can spot insincere and manipulative communication instantly. They also get the point pretty quickly and want to move rapidly from words into actions, which is why the awareness phase should be downsized dramatically for internal

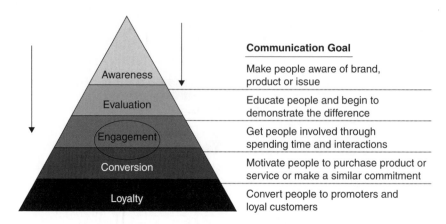

	Communication Goal
Awareness	Make people aware of brand, product or issue
Evaluation	Educate people and begin to demonstrate the difference
Engagement	Get people involved through spending time and interactions
Conversion	Motivate people to purchase product or service or make a similar commitment
Loyalty	Convert people to promoters and loyal customers

FIGURE 7   **Inverting the sales funnel – employee communication flow**

audiences and the bulk of the time, effort and budget invested on involvement, engagement, conversion and loyalty-building activity: *"We get it already, now what does it mean in practice and what's in it for me."*

Employees easily detect conscripted brand decoys and "stool pigeons" used to lure them into compliance against their instincts even more easily than customers can spot apparent staff "Uncle Toms" posing as the normal face of the business in this now much overdone genre of corporate advertisements.

Consider this quote from Tracy, a long-serving supervisor within one of the leading global financial services brands:

> We used to find out about what the brand strategy was when we were shown an agency produced video of the latest set of adverts. Because the adverts included alleged staff members, we were supposed to relate to them. This was different at first but has become a tired and artificial way of projecting the brand.
>
> The videos never really came with an explanation. Their purpose was supposedly to stop us looking stupid when our friends saw the adverts on the television before we did. There never used to be any link into the brand values and it was usually revealing a world that we, the staff, didn't recognise. It was a bit like those plastic people, the model types in the brochures used to recruit people.
>
> Well, I'm pleased to say that all of that has gone now. We have real people on the website, real staff. There's a panel of people who input to

the brand development work by giving guidance to marketing about what we can realistically achieve during a normal day at work. The adverts are in normal language staff and customers can relate to and we get the chance to explore what the adverts mean in the context of our mission, vision and values long before they air. In fact the values have been folded into our appraisal and competency set and are always referred to in training and induction etc. We no longer have to look up the brand values at appraisal time anymore. We get a chance to play with them and bring them to life.

There's still a lot of room for improvement. We must spend a fortune on the ad campaigns compared to our training budgets and line managers are a lot busier than we used to be as our communications role has increased. Also, we're getting a little tired of advertisements showing supposedly "real" staff when any idiot knows that real life at work isn't like that. But at least they ask for feedback at head office and they do seem to listen.

It's hard to escape the fact that there's still a great deal of message management in internal communication departments. The time would be better spent on assessing comprehension and outcomes rather than craft, volume and inputs. The recent trend toward employing interim internal communicators rather than committing to full-time professionals isn't helping. How can you expect to get under the skin of a culture and develop real relationships with senior players on a three-month contract? But as Tracy's quote forewarns, if organizations resort to pushing internal brand communication cloaked in the trappings of engagement it's akin to washing the car and then parking it under a tree full of dyspeptic pigeons.

The engagement and two-way communication phases need to be expanded dramatically for internal stakeholders. Employees need to have plenty of opportunities to explore assertions made about the brand for themselves and two-way channels to exchange feedback. The more empowered and involved employees feel, the more likely they are to climb the ladder of participation to the point that they start to generate on-brand and on-strategy initiatives under their own steam.

In these relatively empowered days, employees really do resist the conscriptive, prescriptive or inauthentic. In the face of overwhelming odds, this increasingly manifests itself in passive aggressive behavior rather than extroverted acts of aggression. In fact loyal employees

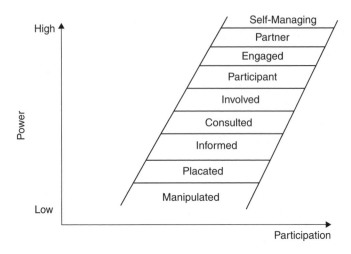

FIGURE 8 **The BY2W ladder of participation model**

may well view it as their duty to be awkward when confronted with a depiction of a brand and culture they simply don't recognize. Persist with a strategy that perpetuates these approaches and the consequences for your brand can quickly move from a steady decline to brand catastrophe.

WHEN ENGAGEMENT TURNS IN ON ITSELF AND HEROES BECOME VILLAINS

As we've spent some time exploring the Everyman employee and the hero or champion tradition, it's only appropriate that we venture into the dark side. In *The Science of Supervillains*, Gresh and Weinberg talk about the need for the hero to triumph as being axiomatic; it's a given. But at the core of their thesis is the need for the hero to struggle. Without a battle against overwhelming odds there's no dramatic tension. This is why the villain so often outclasses the hero and why villains seem to outnumber their counterparts.

If the primary brand champion is predominantly positioned as the CEO or leading executives, not only is the fate of the brand intrinsically linked to their personal career flight path, implying that they really do need to have and maintain the correct trajectory, but it's also hard for these uber heroes to garner sympathy, making it relatively easy for employees to abdicate responsibility. As most change managers will tell you, this scenario often creates a sense of us and him/her/them when things go wrong.

BP certainly struggled when revelations of Lord Browne's private life were forced into the public domain given his high profile. And following this totemic hero tradition at BP, John Browne's successor, Tony Hayward, hitherto relatively unknown, fast became the brand when the Deepwater Horizon disaster struck.

The Virgin brand is heavily dependent on Richard Branson's fate and frame of mind, albeit he works hard to develop and sustain a strong Virgin culture, and Gerald Ratner, Martha Stewart and Robert Maxwell have proven what a single ill-advised phrase or action can do to a brand that is synonymous with your name.

Most brands, however, aren't cults of personality. They are hives, the sum of an intricate chain or community of employees busily, and often unwittingly, keeping the promises made by their marketing functions. Brands live and die on the back of those promises, although arguably when brand advocacy is shared it's a risk that is spread across the broad shoulders of employee engagement and goodwill.

As we all know from the best thrillers, the story of the evolution of most brands reflects a rocky road or heroic journey where fortunes rise and fall, and challenges and threats appear and are conquered, and opportunities spotted and hopefully taken. Think how close the RBS or Royal Bank of Scotland brand came to being arguably one of the top two banking superpowers but for a calamitous takeover of ABN AMRO, spearheaded by Fred Goodwin, coinciding with the collapse of the lending markets.

But as we also know, sometimes the "good guy" isn't all he seems. Sometimes the internal brand custodians, like the angry mob, can turn nasty. If the engagement gap between the leadership and employees grows into a chasm, it can be hard to tell the brand champions from the villains, especially when one group dominates the airwaves and PR machine.

In *Living the Brand*, Ind refers to brand saboteurs, maliciously working actively against the brand idea. The implication is that there are quite a lot of these antiheroes present in most organizations and they are well equipped to cause damage.

I don't altogether buy into the elite force of brand champions implied by Ind's categorization of the branded populace. It stands to reason that I have reservations about the degree of organized premeditation implied by his brand saboteur category as well. I prefer to refer to the extreme saboteur cadre as the Brand Dead, that hardcore minority within most organizations who've simply had enough of the slings and arrows of corporate life, have given up and should really move on for everyone's benefit. In my experience they make up only about 5% of organizations and you probably know who they are.

Brand cynics, however, are far more prevalent. Cynicism is a natural by-product of experience. Skepticism, in fact, is natural and healthy in moderation; it keeps us all on our toes. Cynics, however, have passion and energy. They aren't innately contrary or evil but are usually vociferous because they care about what they perceive to be the true cause. But that energy and passion, if acknowledged rather than ignored and properly channeled through dialog and turned into positive outcomes by being honest about business strategy and brand values, for example, can ultimately be very helpful in providing the brand engagement process with momentum.

Disregard them, however, or attempt to align them with what they perceive to be insincere propaganda about a depiction of the brand they neither like nor trust and they will turn nasty. Turn them into victimized underdogs and these informal leaders can seriously disrupt the brand development effort.

Antiheroes in the eyes of the leaders are often created when employees ironically care enough about the brand to summon up the passion to rebel against actions taken by their leaders which they feel are not in their best interests or those of the company and brand they represent. At the very least they can be disruptive. At the worst they can actively dissuade customers from buying, passively undermine the brand through inaction, or even withdraw their labor completely and strike.

So what happens to brand promises when staff choose industrial action, walk out, strike? The answer isn't as simple as it would first appear.

If we adopt the normal one-eyed approach, the line of the brand Cyclops, and only consider the impact of industrial action on customers, we typically view strikes as financial disasters often leading to short-term disruption and possible loss of market share. They call for an emergency quick fix.

This was certainly the nightmare facing the high street retailer I worked with several Christmases ago which was threatened with strike action when they were at their most vulnerable. It was also the scenario faced by the airline which repeatedly placed process and procedure before people and the telecommunications company which froze employee pay rises yet paid their directors handsome awards.

But when the reasons behind the problems are issues based, then after some relatively simple changes to their internal communications and assiduous negotiation, organizations like the retailer in question often bounce back and quickly recover consumer confidence.

However, if they don't change their internal cultural norms, they're likely to face the same problems time and again. It saddens but doesn't surprise me to see the same organizations facing a repeat of the industrial action when the effects of the emergency measures have worn off.

One of the few benefits of a recession is that customers can be particularly forgiving when the reasons underpinning a spate of industrial action are related to prevailing market conditions. They can also be forgiving when the values the strikers appear to be striving to protect echo their own.

In fact in the eye of the public there's something heroic about the champion of the legacy brand seemingly fighting for fairness with the same passion with which they used to deliver what was, with hindsight, a great service. Because they are perceived by the public as being proud enough of their brand to put their jobs at risk it's not unusual for the villains in the eyes of the senior executives to be portrayed as heroes in the press.

This is especially true when national institution or nostalgia brands like the Royal Mail, London Underground and Cadbury, certain public services, even Woolworths and so-called national airlines, for example, are perceived to be under threat from their own management. The board may well be trying to protect and build brand equity for the greater good but can easily be portrayed as the villains of the piece.

If we respect the factors behind brand equity from the inside out first and foremost, and respect the fact that most employees don't just come to work for a pay check but actually want to care passionately about the brands, the tribes they work for and identify with, employee engagement related brand disasters are far less likely to happen in the first place. And prevention really is much less painful than cure.

Don't be fooled into thinking that strike action is a 1970s phenomenon or a public sector disease. Fujitsu, HP, London Underground, BA, BT, EDS and most high street banks are just a few high-profile brands wrestling with extremely disengaged staff as I write. In each case the strike-mongers are viewed by their management as brand antiheroes.

Strike action is the extreme manifestation of a breakdown in employee engagement. But strikes often actively involve hitherto brand champions.

Yes, strikes project negativity and can look and feel extremely destructive, especially to leaders introducing change. But at least they demonstrate passion and energy, qualities that can potentially be channeled for the greater good. Employees who've switched off yet still show up to work everyday, however, are a much more malignant threat to your brand.

Relationships are rebuildable, but only if the communication channels remain open and everyone involved remembers that communication is more about listening than it is about pushing and managing messages. The trouble that stems from not realizing you had an issue in the first place is much harder to deal with when apathy has become a cultural norm.

Dip into the reporting related to the Fujitsu, Tube, BA or Royal Mail disputes and you'll invariably be met with references to "last ditch talks." The trouble is that within organizations where the relationship between brand and personnel, brand values and organization culture is not appreciated and there's little consultation and feedback, the dialog is always the last resort.

Strikes are usually simplified in the press as clashes of intransigent polar extremes: management vs. workers, greed vs. survival, heroes vs. villains. But they're a lot more complicated than the caricatures of greasy pinstripes vs. blue collar table bashers suggest.

Consider the problems faced by one of the UK's largest brands, the Royal Mail. On the face of it the spate of recent disputes can be seen as the death throes resulting from the once irresistible force of New Labour's spin doctors meeting the formerly immovable object of trade unionism. But talk to the real brand champions, the ordinary postman or even customer in the street (or behind the letterbox), and this dispute is about so much more. It's about a fight for identity by employees who are emotionally connected with a brand which they, and their customers, see as a national institution. It's about culture, "the way things get done around here," and workers resisting the evil march of automation, which experience tells us may slash cost off the bottom line but does not guarantee better customer service or an improved quality of life (anyone remember the days of second post and trustworthy postal staff?).

In short, it's a brand battleground that reflects a range of hot social issues and topics, including culture, values and identity.

The £11.5bn takeover of another so-called British brand institution, Cadbury, by US food brand Kraft is another case in point. The Quaker founding fathers of Cadbury, who formed the business in 1824, famously took a holistic approach to the application of their ideology. They created the utopian Bournville village in England's Midlands for Cadbury staff where the Cadbury values transcended the brand to become a social manifesto. Cadbury literally managed a society. Leafy Bournville with its village greens and cricket pavilions was even recently voted the best place to live in Britain.

When a brand like Cadbury comes under threat of takeover, it easily becomes an attack on the national identity, the host country's way of life. It's relatively easy to depict an assault on the brand as an attack on a series of communities, regardless of the commercial business case. The same techniques used to sell their "feel good" confectionary in their product range is easily subverted to contrast the motives of Kraft with the nostalgic yearning for halcyon days, a lost way of life and a vanishing idyll in the minds of Cadbury's staff and customers. The acquisitive entity easily becomes the threatening, dark shadow. Powerful stuff this brand equity.

The reporting of the Cadbury/Kraft takeover plans conjured up images and phrases more akin to the immigration and imperialism debate and wartime rhetoric than to the inevitable consequences of capitalism. Cadbury's employees were feted as virtual anti-imperialist, rebel heroes, the romantic resistance movement.

Much of the criticism of Kraft following the takeover surrounded apparent pledges made to retain Cadbury's 400-strong Somerdale factory. These apparent pledges were reversed once the deal was done.

The vitriol centered on Irene Rosenfeld, the boss of Kraft. She has been called "incompetent" by the unions over pledges to protect the 400 employees at the Somerdale factory and she didn't win any popularity contests when it was revealed that Rosenfeld was awarded a 40% pay rise, to $17mn, for brokering the deal yet had not even been seen at the factories. This was contrasted with the benevolence, morality and corporate social responsibility of the Quaker founding fathers.

A particularly unfavorable impression was created when, instead of traveling to London herself, Rosenfeld delegated her corporate affairs director to face an all-party Commons business select committee in March 2010 that wanted to get to the bottom of the much publicized unrest post-takeover. Hardly the behavior of a hero leader. Six months after the takeover she still hadn't visited the UK plants.

Regardless of the business benefits of the takeover, Rosenfeld quickly went from aspirant brand champion to Shadow then Mask (in Campbell's terminology). She became a supervillain overnight because she had inadvertently placed herself in direct opposition to the true Cadbury brand champions, the people on the shop floor not the suits in the board room.

She also managed to divert attention away from the true root cause of employee discontentment. In the reporting surrounding the takeover, there was little mention made of the fact that it was actually the Cadbury board who came up with the plan to relocate operations to Poland in the first place. There was also very little mention made of the fact that the Cadbury board had long since left behind their Quaker roots and that Cadbury had an acquisitive past of its own, subsuming brands like the similarly principled Frys into the brand with little assimilation of the Frys values.

It is ironic that writing in *The Daily Telegraph* just before the Kraft deal closed, Sir Dominic and Sir Adrian Cadbury said:

> *In the context of a bid, the high percentage that fail to live up to the claims of the bidder are well documented. The risks of relative failure in takeovers are therefore clear. Those risks are considerably increased if the bidder fails to win the loyalty and support of the employees on whom the continuing fortunes of the enterprise depend.*

There's significant evidence to suggest that the Cadbury family had already lost the support of their staff when they outsourced the production to Poland, despite the passion and loyalty the staff had shown to the brand and the founding values and ideals.

Viewed objectively, not only was the Cadbury takeover inevitable and the key issues hardly of Kraft's making, given that the efficiency strategy was well under way before they came on the scene, but the takeover could also potentially benefit the employees in the long term. By misjudging the power of the employees, their loyalty and passion for the Cadbury brand and by failing to prioritize mentor leaders and line managers within Cadbury, Kraft has made the takeover a great deal more difficult than it should have been. Kraft has inadvertently taken on the supervillain mantle.

There are many positives about the takeover that have been lost in translation and frankly bad management. Kraft would be foolish to undermine the Cadbury brand, having paid so much to acquire it. The Kraft takeover of French brand Danone, for example, has resulted in additional investment in France and can hardly be said to have diluted the brand.

But consider the CEMEX case study in contrast and their attitude to brand development through acquisition versus the way the Cadbury employees have been treated by both sets of directors.

Naturally there will be challenges, most importantly leadership issues as well as culture development threats and opportunities. The Kraft executives will now need to understand the people and behavioral assets they've acquired, reconfigure the employee engagement and internal communication function and find ways to reconcile the legacy Cadbury values with their own. At the moment their CEO is setting a less than inspiring example and a worryingly high number of key Cadbury leaders, the mentors within the Cadbury empire, are moving on under cover of the chaos.

Most importantly, the Cadbury employees will have to be convinced of the benefits and enticed to re-engage with the "third way" that will have to emerge from the equation of splicing together two mega brands. But it can be done. The alternative isn't very palatable, as the explosive cocktail of disenchanted staff and almost nationalistic zeal is a potent one, especially when the passion and energy generated are misdirected.

As someone who specializes in helping organizations manage brands from within I've been called upon to help avert a number of high-profile strikes in the past five years. Despite the challenge, it's never something I particularly look forward to, largely because it's seldom a pleasant process.

In each of the cases I've been involved with the core issue wasn't about pay and rations despite the fact that these are usually cited. Strikes are usually about fundamental communication root causes like listening, consultation and disenchanted staff who feel their managers are no longer connected with the values they believe their brand represents. They're often about loss of trust and the creation of "us vs. them" caricatures with both sides claiming the brand superhero

T-shirts and positioning the others as the villains when ironically they usually have the same interests in mind.

In the disputes I have been involved with, there were differing degrees of pain involved but, eventually, in each case catastrophe was averted through:

- reopening communication channels
- revisiting core values to reach common ground
- repositioning change as another stage in the continuing evolution of the brand
- reexamining the legacy of the organization and appreciating the contributions of the predecessors
- working on a jointly crafted vision and mission
- re-evaluating the brand and related values
- repositioning the brand and developing empathy for the perceptions both parties had of the brand, which had somehow moved into opposite camps
- insisting on the reinstatement of respect (at least for the entitlement to a point of view) and active listening
- adoption of the brand values to guide and govern discussions
- understanding the current culture and agreeing a desired future culture together
- reconfiguring internal communication approaches and channels

Interestingly, a couple of the situations I've faced recently have been within the higher education sector where the head teacher, the board appointed superhero sent to usher the organization into the new century, has had to adopt new notions of commercialism and the challenge of creating a brand that was fit for modern purpose. Even the use of the term "brand" has attracted a hostile response.

Both heads clashed with backward-looking idealists who viewed teaching very differently. They didn't see the organization as a business, or a brand for that matter. Unfortunately these idealists also happened to include many of the best teachers, who couldn't see the irony of actively turning away new students who tried to cross picket lines during the enrolment process.

Both parties were equally passionate; both were products of their respective times, but it wasn't possible for the red and blue flags to fly over the building simultaneously. What they were able to do eventually, however, was recognize and respect respective passions and skill sets, ultimately come to an understanding about the origins and journey of the organization, reinvent the notion of a brand and pay due homage to their legacy while improving the quality and security of the Ordinary World.

Respect for legacy is so often an underestimated part of any change process. It involves acknowledging and honoring the forebears, the custodians of the ordinary world, enough to articulate and appreciate their contribution before moving on. It means tapping into the passion of the "founding fathers" and militants to move forward productively together in the best interests of the organization, the brand.

Both brands in question are still evolving and it has been extremely difficult to initiate change. But at least the strikes have stopped; some of the ringleaders have eventually become champions of the refreshed brand; the communication has lost most of its destructive and often childish edge and takes place behind closed doors rather than in obstructive third-party forums.

Six years ago I was working with British Airways helping to bridge an engagement gap which had gradually grown between staff and managers as the organization attempted to implement policy and process changes which many employees deemed to be out of tune with their corporate culture.

Around the same period I worked with the Royal Mail as the directors wrestled with a hugely ambitious change program and were anxious to create an internal culture fit for purpose.

Since then millions have been spent on advertising and core process redesign in each case, yet their employee engagement and culture development budgets have not followed suit. Is it a coincidence that industrial action is still never far from the surface?

The advent of social media has brought an added dimension to disputes of this nature, especially given the difficulty large corporate machines have in controlling the use of these media and the fact that the most adept users are likely to reside on the side of the skirmishers rather than the big battalions.

In an article I co-authored for the Chartered Institute of PR's Inside function, of which I'm a UK advisory board member, Sean Trainor and Social Media expert Euan Semple offer some telling contributions about the attitude of BA's CEO, Willie Walsh, during the latest spate of industrial action. Says Sean:

I don't want to criticise his approach to union negotiations, regulatory affairs and government relations but I do wonder what key messages his bullish standoff position sends out to the wider audience, especially his employees. There is definitely an air of "My business would be better off without all these people getting in my way." Be careful what you wish for Willie.

Anti-social media

When you look at what Derek Simpson tweeted during negotiations it was pretty innocuous, so why did Willie choose to take great issue with them?

Was it because he was angry that nobody in his team was monitoring and knocking on the door to warn him what was happening? Or was it because it highlighted that the unions tend to be adept at getting out simple messages in a timely way to their members, and social media tools are allowing them to be even more sophisticated? An employee of another company in the transport sector told us that during a strike in the US they all joined and followed the union's social media stuff because that was where they got the most up-to-date information.

Increasingly there is a gap between those who adopt social media tools and those who don't. There will always be a gap, what's important is how we deal with it, respecting whatever camp people are in. Just as we shouldn't rubbish the early adopters (even if they make a few mistakes along the way) we should respect those people who don't get it, not rub their noses in it but help them to catch up.

He recalls his experience of meetings at the BBC five years ago where:

one half of the room were alluding to extra information, back stories and context that they were aware of due to following online conversations while the other half of the room had no idea what we were talking about. Unlike Unite, the BBC unions were slow to get involved, maybe they had too much to lose by upsetting the cosy dance they had enjoyed for years with HR!

Strike action is seldom the product of sudden policy and personnel changes or the work of malicious supervillains hell bent on destruction for the sake of it.

These are seldom the root cause but are often the corporate straw which breaks the back of employee goodwill.

People care more about the brands they work for than you may think.

Culture, the way people do things within the organizations that support those brands, is probably the most important determinant of brand performance.

If you agree that there's some sense in this argument, then ask yourself:

- who and where are your chief engagement officers?
- how would you describe the relationship between Marketing and HR?
- how professional and fleet of foot is your internal communication function?
- what measures are you taking to clarify your employer brand?
- what attempts are you making to engage and manage your talent?
- are you regularly enquiring into how engaged people are with the business and acting on the results?

Regardless of whether an actual strike is likely at your organization, it's certainly worth spending some time understanding the true DNA of your brand. If you don't know what brand engagement is worth, especially in the lean times, consider whether you can you risk your employees deserting their posts or, even worse, disengaged staff continuing to represent your brand.

Leaked papers, disgruntled customers or market intelligence anyone?

To summarize:

Brand engagement is largely about authentic communication. Authentic communication creates the conditions in which true brand champions thrive. Brand champions are worth more than their weight in gold, largely because they:

- are volunteers rather than conscripts and therefore work harder
- lead with their actions rather than words
- bring the brand values to life
- are usually leaders rather than managers
- are as attractive to their peers as they are to staff and customers

Take them for granted and don't give them a voice, however, and your brand champions can quickly change outfits and become potent adversaries.

But you can't track your brand champions down through auditions or handpick them from the C suite. You have to enter their territory. And they tend to be very busy people.

PART 3

BRAND SUPERHEROES UNCOVERED

IS IT A BIRD? IS IT A PLANE? NO IT'S STAN FROM ACCOUNTS

You don't have to have a postgraduate degree in the legacy of Marvel Comics or be a devotee of storytelling gurus like Joseph Campbell to appreciate the link between the attractiveness of heroic figures in popular culture and testing social circumstances. It's no great surprise that the Golden Age of superhero comics coincided with a catastrophic world war.

Michael Chabon captures the spirit of this Golden Age in the excellent Pulitzer Prize-winning *The Amazing Adventures of Kavalier & Clay,* in which his two protagonists create the fictional character The Escapist. Exiled far from the actual fighting, an alter ego is their only way of fighting the Nazis, the antithesis of their core values.

Chabon juxtaposes tragedy with commercialism and the rise of the sense-making and empowering notion that truth somehow lies at the intersection of harsh reality and comic book fantasy. *The Escapist* comic book strip about a Nazi-busting savior eventually earns the lead characters fame and fortune. But can their fictional counterpart solve the very real problems they face in their real life dramas played out against the dark backdrop in which the novel is set? The tension is in the interplay between fantasy and social reality. But in the end it's the multidimensional human story that turns out to be stranger than fiction. It is in real life, beyond the façade, where the real heroes are eventually to be found.

It's rather like that in corporate land, isn't it? Corporate communication functions work hard to remove emotion from the stories they tell and the words they use. But truth and the real action take place on the vibrant front line.

Following the recent collapse of the western banking industry and a stock market bloodbath characterized by short selling and cutthroat avarice, today's employees can't be blamed for looking around for a superhero or two to provide reassurance, leadership and support. Corporate reality has been pretty unpalatable at times. So can anyone blame Joe and Janet public for searching the skies for a savior in primary colors when this commercial turmoil takes place amidst scandals affecting politicians and religious and other establishment figures worldwide? But in the workaday real time of corporate reality when the "critical points of inflection" arrive, it's the Everyman employee who has to knuckle down and make a difference.

It may be popularity polls and share prices rather than bombs that have dropped in recent times but as world and corporate leaders struggle with economic crises who wouldn't welcome a caped crusader who could clear tall buildings in a single bound? If you could truly trust them and they also had the answer to the boom-and-bust corporate culture plumping out their codpieces, all the better.

In the very real world of organizations and commerce, however, we're more likely to bump into a bumbling Clark Kent, a nerdy Bruce Banner or a super slick Bruce Wayne than a Super or Bat man. But that's a good thing. Individual heroes are few and far between, and brand heroes seldom reside in the C suite. As *Pale Rider*, *A Fistful of Dollars* and so many of the movies of Clint Eastwood often show us, permanent change isn't driven by a single hero; it doesn't happen until Everyman and the "villagers" step forward to be counted. Brand heroes too are most likely to live and work around us in the corporate village every day. So there's hope for us all.

True brand champions are the plodding police officers, the multi-shift doctors, the firefighters, the dedicated teachers. But they are also the gray-suited insurance underwriters, personal assistants, customer contact staff and copywriters. They're often the little people who are able to rise above the universal and altogether natural concern for the self and put the needs of others first in their list of priorities because, in the long run, it makes the workplace a more rewarding environment in which to do business.

They too fight for health, safety, growth, justice, liberty, excellence and other values in their own modest way. But unlike their comic book counterparts, they usually don't have special powers and they're not forced or compelled to heroic acts by their performance contracts. They do it because they largely believe that we're on this planet for a good time not a long time whether we're at work or not. And when they do happen to epitomize the brand, it's because, in the main, they choose to.

Brand champions, contrary to the marketing spin, are usually self-electing rather than made that way by corporate programs, internal marketing or desperate alignment. Too many people have attended the course where the opening message is

Remember, the key to sales success is mastering insincerity

to care too much about messages from Marketing about their con-scripted brand ambassadorial duties.

Even if they don't always appreciate it, organizations count on there being enough of these ordinary superheroes in sensible shoes quietly making a stand for truth, justice and values within the corporate rank and file. But if you care enough to look out for them, how exactly do you spot them given they aren't likely to be wearing their pants over their tights and probably choose not to sport a natty cape or tiara?

Like any person, a brand has a physical "body": in P&G's case, the products and/or services it provides. Also, like a person, a brand has a name, a personality, character and a reputation.

Like a person, you can respect, like and even love a brand. You can think of it as a deep personal friend, or merely an acquaintance. You can view it as dependable or undependable; principled or opportunistic; caring or capricious. Just as you like to be around certain people and not others, so also do you like to be with certain brands and not others.

Also, like a person, a brand must mature and change its product over time. But its character, and core beliefs shouldn't change. Neither should its fundamental personality and outlook on life. People have character...so do brands. A person's character flows from his/her integrity: the ability to deliver under pressure, the willingness to do what is right rather than what is expedient. You judge a person's character by his/her past performance and the way he/she thinks and acts in both good times, and especially bad.

The same are true of brands.

Robert Blanchard, former P&G executive,
from *Parting Essay*, July 1999

WHAT DOES AN ENGAGED BRAND CHAMPION LOOK LIKE?

If anyone is prepared to willingly bear a brand on their breast there's a fair chance, unless they're being ironic, that they're going to be substantially engaged with that brand. But could you pick one out of a lineup if they weren't made to wear silly badges or stars or to suffer the alienating ignominy of having their photo in the lobby?

While there are variations and eccentricities, having run countless workshops across sectors and having helped build diagnostic tools to identify the levers of employee engagement backed up by the cross-sector 2005 BY2W employee engagement research project, I would suggest that the most common traits exhibited by engaged employees are summed up by the ironic acronym **RIPE:**

Qualities of engaged employees
- **Receptive** (they are open to opportunities to be involved)
- **Involved** (they are part of the program not recipients of it)
- **Proactive** (they innovate without being asked)
- **Energized** (they do more things)

Outcomes
- **Achievers** (the things they do tend to be fruitful)
- **Advocates** (they are proud and happy and actively recommend the brand)

Write down a list of the ten people you would think of when you're asked to define a brand role model, a brand champion, and there's little doubt they will possess these characteristics. Delve beneath the surface of the UK's *Times* Best 100 Companies poll and you'll encounter these characters and characteristics or employees with RIPE credentials. Attend a conference populated by representatives from a range of brands and you'll be able to distinguish the attendees from organizations where brand champions thrive as their RIPE credentials will be clear.

Having worked with a number of organizations in the top 25 (including MSDW, ZFS and Orange) I can confirm that in each case:

- the top team were advocates of a culture-led approach to brand management
- they developed a very clear business case for change
- they understood the current culture and were clear about the desired future culture
- they involved and engaged all employees in the development of a compelling story about the evolution of the business
- they "professionalized" their internal communication function and ensured that line managers in particular were skilled communicators
- they insisted on partnerships between the external and internal facing communication/engagement functions

Doesn't sound anything like where you work?
Still feel RIPE can only be applied to fruit?
Still can't spot the superheroes?

Well next time there's a corporate crisis just pause for a second and watch. Try and look beyond the chaos that the emails from the CEO and army of middle managers are creating and listen through the double speak and noise. Now consider why the otherwise unassuming and bespectacled Debbie from IT always grabs her coat and heads for the stationery cupboard when the going gets tough. Someone, after all, is keeping the supervillains at bay and the systems running;

someone is keeping their head at least while all around you are losing theirs.

SO WHERE ARE THE SUPERHEROES?

The compelling case for the first line supervisor

Brand champions don't tend to come with a unified rank. Yes there are the uber brand champions in the C suite of the Branson, Gates and Jobs guise. But lucky for Richard, Bill, Steve and co., brand champions appear at all levels. In *Brand Engagement,* however, I do make a particular case for the *chief engagement officer* or ceo as the pivotal communicator within the modern business.

Overwhelmingly, chief engagement officers tend to be first line managers.

In a 2009 Bring Yourself 2 Work poll of 1000 representatives from over 700 companies, they answered the question "Who is the most important internal communicator in your organization?" as follows:

- The HR Director (2%)
- The CEO (23%)
- My line manager (27%)
- My department head (48%)
- The Marketing Director (0%)

But when we asked the same people the question "Who is the most useful internal communicator in your organization?" the results were very different:

- The HR Director (4%)
- The CEO (12%)
- My line manager (57%)
- My department head (27%)
- The Marketing Director (0%)

Clearly status and practicality are two very different things.

This shouldn't come as a great surprise even if it will come as something of a shock for the Marketing department. But I wonder how highly internal communication functions generally prioritize line managers in their strategies. The first line manager population are the people who, in modern businesses, are predominantly responsible for connecting the business with the people on a day-to-day basis. I've seen nothing since in the millions of soundbites about godlike CEOs and so-called liberating, stand alone new media, social media and technology to convince me otherwise. Funky technology is fun and is useful if well applied but there's no substitute for a pulse, voice, nurturing manner and active, attentive set of ears.

In an age where process reengineering has removed layers of leadership and customer relationship managers have been upstaged by call centers, where social media solutions are being touted as communications nirvana and face-to-face communication is somehow seen as old-fashioned, the Everyman first line manager and supervisor has literally never been so important. He/she is the vital link in the chain between the brand promise and the delivery of that promise because he/she is primarily responsible for engaging the vast majority of the workforce with the core purpose, vision, mission and values of the organization. Lasting brand engagement doesn't happen at grandstand events alone.

It's a fact that the organization's people processes, the core engagement channels such as performance management, training and development, communication and recruitment, thrive or wither away at the line manager's desk not in the HR department. The organization's culture is usually typified by them. They are, to all intents and purposes, the bridge between the legacy of the business and the stories people will be telling about the business in the future.

In the challenging and entertaining *Superheroes and Philosophy*, the prolific philosopher Tom Morris anachronistically talks about the reason for and importance of dualities in the world of superheroes. He writes about how normal people, when fulfilling challenging roles during the journey through life, often adopt different modes of identity to cope with the challenge. But businesses should be encouraging authenticity, looking for the real person, not forcing their line managers to adopt alter egos.

"It's hard not to become an arsehole when you're first given the responsibility to line manage so many staff." This line, from a young supervisor at the challenger brand egg, is one of my favorite quotes as it bluntly sums up one of the key leadership challenges first line managers face – remaining true to themselves and encouraging their people to keep it real.

THE HERO AND THE MASK

Astute line managers are aware of the associations that come with pointless badges of authority. They invest time and effort in uncovering, coaching and nurturing their brand champions rather than managing initiative out of them. They don't let rank and the trappings of office get in the way.

Academics dress in a certain way to signal their vocation, to conform; so do power-dressing executives. Comic book superheroes, as we know, are given dual identities where the difference between the everyday persona and work persona is exaggerated to emphasize, through contrast, their heroic qualities.

Consider this brief list:

Superhero persona	Social persona
Spider-Man	geekie Peter Parker
The Hulk	bookish scientist Bruce Banner
Batman	roguish millionaire Bruce Wayne
Wonder Woman	straight-laced Diana Prince

And let's not forget that head boy of the bunch, the alpha male boy scout in spandex, Superman, and his alter ego, the bumbling and awkward journalist Clark Kent.

Of course those talented folk at Marvel, DC and so on are subverting the Everyman vs. superhero relationship. They are suggesting that the Everyman persona is the mask the heroes choose to wear to cope with what is for them the challenge of dealing with the extraordinary circumstance of daily life without frightening the horses. It is a subtle form of propaganda to reassure the general populace that exceptional good guys are amongst them despite the dark days. But it is also a barely subtle form of propaganda encouraging normal people to look for superhero qualities in themselves (even less subtle in the hugely popular *Watchmen* strip).

Isn't it just a little bit liberating to at least adopt an appreciative belief that in the workplace, beneath the exterior of even the most unspectacular member of staff, there's a potential brand superhero waiting to be discovered? Yet oddly enough the sterile "staff member of the month" models used in corporate literature to exemplify heroic employees often have the opposite effect on employees and potential recruits.

But even though it's tough for fictional superheroes to blend in as all powerful aliens or superhuman products of freakish genetic accidents, the schizophrenia experienced by the workaday Everyman is arguably more extreme than that of their comic book counterparts. For not only does the average employee come under pressure to maintain the dual identities of the work me and home me like their comic book counterparts, but there's also an added dimension. Most of us have an extra layer, a veiled semi-vocational me through which we express our interests, beliefs and values. What's fascinating is that this extra dimension more often than not is meeting needs that simply aren't addressed in the workplace and expressing values, beliefs, passions, skills and attributes that go unrecognized at the office.

If you reflect for a minute I'm sure you'll agree that in most workplaces it is not unusual to see the following:

Social persona	Needs driven/ organizational persona	Voluntary persona
Dave Reilly	Bank clerk	Sergeant in the Territorial Army
Sally Seeker	Accountant	RSPCA volunteer
Adena Cheeseman	Director	Charity van driver
Ruth Double	Social worker	Rugby referee

What does this mean? Well, however you look at it there's a great deal of unexplored potential for engaging more effectively, getting more from people and gaining increased commitment if we take the trouble to understand this third dimension and encourage its expression in the workplace. As Nicholas Ind puts it, *"An employee can be the same person outside of the organization and inside."* So what's getting in the way?

Remember, as the work of Joseph Campbell shows, the mask is seldom imbued with positive characteristics. The Mask is the antithesis of authenticity, and we've already explored how important authenticity is as one of the cornerstones of trust and employee engagement in traditional narratives. I believe brand communication should encourage a gentle unmasking. And it's predominantly the first line manager who can create an environment in which it's safe to cut the strings holding it in place.

83

Scratch the surface of the workaday employee and, just like Clark Kent, there's a fair chance you'll find positive qualities and values they are somehow forced to suppress at work. The work culture is undoubtedly stifling their true potential and failing to truly engage them as a result. In short, the Everyman employee has greater heroic potential. The trick is to explore what shape that potential takes by enabling them to be themselves rather than force your version of a cape and insignia on them and expect them to want to jump from corporate HQ and fly.

DISCOVERING YOUR INNER SUPERHERO

There are many engaging tools and techniques you can explore to help employees uncover or rediscover and then tap into the potential superhero within. A couple which I find are consistently a low-cost hit are *the heraldic shield* and *design a brand champion* exercises.

Key to the success of both is:

- the creation of a context (how this fits into the story of the evolution of the brand, where they fit in and why the business is doing this)
- an understanding of objectives (what are we looking to get out of this? and what's in it for me?)
- an appreciation that brands are 80% about behaviors and 20% about the physical trappings, so change isn't about rearranging the chairs
- reference to the organization's core values to create the informal rules and set boundaries

Other than that, sympathetic facilitation, involving an "I'll show you mine if you show me yours" attitude, usually generates the required levels of trust and engagement. Unfailingly, people love the chance to suspend their disbelief, throw off formality and, in a safe place, play.

My heraldic shield

The premise behind this exercise is that people, whether from the legacy of romantic writing or from the screen and stage, are largely familiar with the notion of family crests, one of the earliest examples of personal branding and differentiation. They are largely comfortable with the use of insignia and imagery to sum up the values and qualities associated with a unit, a group, which help define their identity, even if they haven't made the association between individual and corporate brand.

This exercise is particularly useful if employed as part of a change journey (as we explored in Part 1), a brand refresh or reevaluation, or any program or intervention where participants are encouraged to throw away the shackles of normal office life, open their minds and embark on a transformational adventure. It's also energizing, bonding and a lot of fun.

We engage participants by encouraging them to reflect on the values they hold dear in both worlds and turn these into simple images, and then we invite them to capture the output using the simple device of inventing their own heraldry or brand. They are then invited to reveal their shield and tell the group the stories which are associated with their choices.

What the participant group is doing together is creating a character, a paper-based avatar if you will, which exists in a safe place and through which they can explore more about each other, the individual, their challenges, hopes, fears and importantly their values, than they otherwise would.

As a way of embedding the learnings from the exercise and hopefully marking their commitment to the group, participants can then be encouraged to literally pin their personalized shields to a communal wall of commitment at the end of the process. This is synonymous with crossing the threshold and committing to change. But the brand heroes only commit if they are willing to support the cause in question. The core premise is that this wall of commitment (the egg at Argos, aeroplane at Easyjet, map at NITB, runway at Zurich, tree at CFS (refer Figure 9) and so on) becomes an organizational totem, a symbol of the beliefs, values and commitment of the individuals that collectively underpin the organization's brand. It sounds a little melodramatic, almost clichéd and trite for some tastes, but it works. It's simple enough but a very powerful way of connecting people back to the personal origins of brand and the potential power of the corporate brand.

It's important that the participants are asked to revisit this exercise once they have had the chance to explore the brand values of their organization and the behaviors associated with them. It is then possible to invite them to repeat the process, this time reflecting on what the brand values mean to them relative to their own value set.

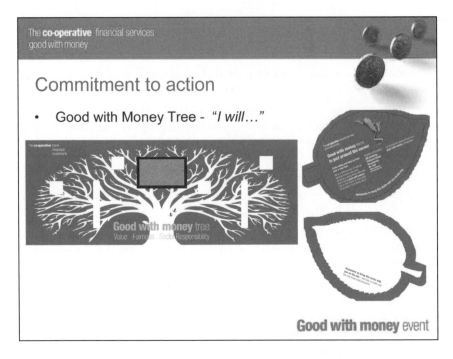

FIGURE 9   **The CFS tree of commitment, linking personal and organizational**
values

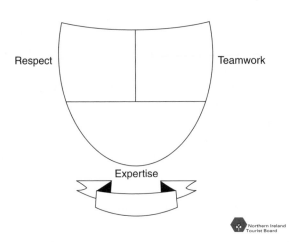

FIGURE 10   **The heraldic shield template populated with the NITB values**

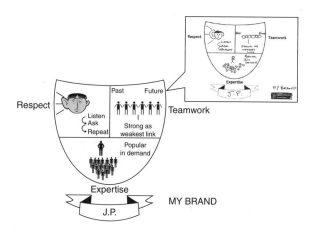

FIGURE 11   **A completed heraldic shield linking brand and individual values**

In one example, the line manager who participated held up his shield and gave a fairly engaging "presentation" about the values and how they applied to his role at the office. He talked us through the way he relates to the brand by listening more than talking, focusing much of his time on ensuring that all of his team are as well informed and well developed as the rest and so on. He then moved from engaging to compelling when he told the story of his home life and caring for his disabled child, applying each of the values to everyday scenarios and painting a vivid picture of his passion and priorities. What could have been an interesting but forgettable cameo from an unassuming chief engagement officer became an impactful, bonding and memorable piece of engaging communication which brought the values to life for his colleagues.

In another example, a senior executive started talking about the organization values associated with safety when he stopped and paused for a couple of minutes. It was clear that he wasn't happy churning out the usual "party line" and eventually he chose to tell a story instead.

He took the group back to the first week he joined the company and how one of his colleagues had witnessed an accident which resulted in a fatality. He described the impact it had on even the most hard nosed of his colleagues and how a workmate had broken down when clearing away his friend's personal effects. The story had more impact than all the pie charts and bar graphs in the world or an encyclopedia full of words. He finished his session by writing two initials under the safety sign. As a result of brave contributions like this the reengagement program based around line managers was extremely successful and helped transform the quality of their internal communication.

The gradual unveiling of alter egos isn't always this dramatic but I can recall checkout girls who turned out to be trainee lawyers, hardware store assistants who were former teachers, and Olympic athletes masquerading as marketing managers.

Ideally, having undertaken the heraldic shield exercise, we usually take matters a stage further and ask participants to continue to extend the brand development metaphor. We ask them to consider their shields as the insignia for a new brand superhero. As a bit of fun we ask them to anticipate the brand development journey and the role they will play and then ask them to design the rest of the outfit as if they were literally equipping themselves for the particular challenges they face back at work.

Yes, it's asking people to suspend their disbelief and have fun but there's a serious purpose. In effect we're creating brand superheroes to meet the very real daily challenges they face as representatives (if not ambassadors) of the corporate brand to which they have all subscribed as employees. The process of creating these Everyman heroes is illuminating, as the license it bestows on the participants always yields enlightening outcomes.

Design a brand superhero

Superheroes seldom fail to ignite something dynamic in the creative mind in a fun, fantastical and nonthreatening way. We're all familiar with champions in one form or another, even if we haven't read the comic books, and have doubtless adopted the guise of our heroes, wherever they come from, in role-playing games as children. So why should we pretend that the fun begins and ends in childhood?

Superheroes can seemingly do things ordinary people can't do. They have unique powers and abilities that allow them to overcome the very problems that gall us mere mortals and more. They look like everyday folk but have superhuman, fantastic, extraordinary abilities. They wear special costumes with snazzy hidden gizmos and ingenious, funky gadgets. Who hasn't daydreamed at some stage or other about what they would do if they had superhero powers?

The exciting act of asking people to design their own "what if?" brand superhero who could deal with the everyday challenges they face allows employees to be critical and appreciative at once. They are liberated within the safe space created by the game and allowed and empowered to move beyond normal constraints, to think creatively, to have fun and hopefully to make an intimate connection between the corporate brand, their role and their own values.

This very straightforward design exercise is normally prefaced by a simple brainstorm in which the participants are asked to picture:

- the story of their career to date and key milestones
- challenges they have overcome along the way
- people in their past who have helped them and their characteristics (mentors and archetypes)
- "villains" who've attempted to foil them and their characteristics (archetypes and masks)
- the personal strengths they have shown
- the values they project and defend (and to pick the top three)
- challenges they face in their roles
- opportunities available to them
- what would compel them to act differently and confront problems and issues

They are then asked to rank the top three challenges and grade them, simply by drawing a balloon around the words to reflect the scale and impact of the issue.

The participants consider their role and the challenges they face. They reflect on their answers to the questions above and come up with a name for their brand superhero. There's clearly no right or wrong invention but past brand superheroes have included:

- T&T Girl (front of house role)
- The Customer Avenger (complaint handler)
- The Terminator (HR administrator)
- Dr. Dog's Body (personal assistant)
- Repo Man (call center salesman targeting customer recovery)
- The Intersection (line manager)
- The Matrix (IT support)
- Dinnie Dropoff (health and safety officer with a strong sense of humor and Celtic bent)

As with a lot of the best things in life, tongues are clearly wedged firmly in cheeks for the greater part (with some notable exceptions), but it's a lighthearted way to get people talking about the brand, what it means to them and the challenges they face, without having to come over "all corporate."

The next stage is to ask the participants to equip their superhero:

- with a crest bearing their organization's brand values
- with an appropriate uniform/livery
- with the qualities needed to bring those values to life
- with superpowers and characteristics that help in the quest to live those values

Suddenly a group of help desk associates in a call center start opening up about the unique attributes that get them through the day, the techniques they silently employ to combat customer drop-off or prevent contract terminations or to deal with complaints.

Direct sales assistants share skills relating to multitasking, motivation in the face of adversity and persuasion, and how to keep their identities secret when encountering unwanted probing questions from third parties.

Executive assistants reflect on ways to listen but not be seen, to multitask, to deal with difficult people and to change chameleon-like into different personae to reflect moods and tempers. And line managers give insights into what it's really like being the eyes, ears and

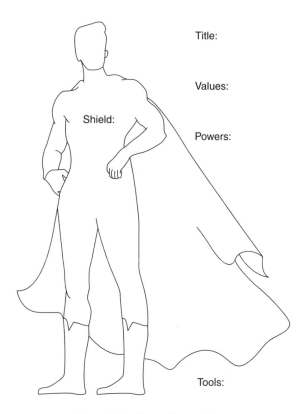

Title:

Values:

Shield:

Powers:

Tools:

FIGURE 12   **One of the brand superhero templates**

voice of the organization, manage multiple stakeholders, pour oil on choppy water and so on.

The Super Project Coordinator exercise helped Adam, his inventor, not only show off his drawing skills (he redesigned the template), but also open up about his love of the frontline aspects of his job. He apparently thrived on meeting clients and representing the company as a "creative." He was very proud of the brand he represented but felt besieged at times by the administrative elements of his role.

To combat what he perceived as random demands from the consultants and directors he works with, he invented a surprisingly vulnerable hero with the broad shoulders and square chin as well as thick skin he already visualized daily when he had to take the blows. He also revealed a surprising sensitivity to the jealousy of his colleagues,

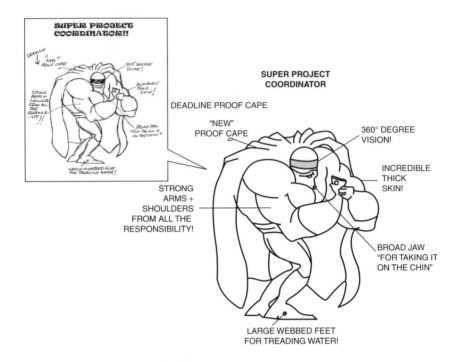

FIGURE 13   **An example of a brand superhero – the Super Project Coordinator**

whom he perceived as resenting his time out of the office, and to the fact that this was affecting communication within the team and getting in the way of sharing best practices.

The amusing conversation that followed in the plenary group led to some fundamental changes to the way he interacted with his peers and how his colleagues related to him in return. He was open to constructive suggestions which eventually led to improved work scheduling and cooperation between team members. It also resulted in an agreement to enter into a League of Superheroes with his other project team members, who, after attending the workshop and drawing up their own brand characters, agreed to merge "superpowers" for the common cause. Their line manager had to work hard to ensure that he didn't become the supervillain in the piece and received some valuable feedback on the qualities he needed to enhance in the best interests of harmony within the League.

We've had similar results in call center environments where whole teams have created superhero liveries for their part of the office, renamed meeting rooms and redesigned processes to bring the values to life and to "defend the brand." Whoever said brand management was a chore?

Sure the ideas that stem from this exercise are usually out in the fantasy stratosphere somewhere just past planet Krypton. But it does get people talking about common challenges and coping strategies (even the very senior ones). It never fails to spark fresh approaches and new ways of working that are essentially "on brand" and can be tempered to match most change scenarios:

Design the superhero to champion our re-brand
- what would the ideal change agent look like?
- what sort of challenges would they have to face?
- how does this fit into the story of the evolution of our brand?
- if you were recruiting a superhero to complement our team, what would he/she look like?

The Projecto character was the alter ego confession of a project manager in an information services organization. Typically systematic, the inventor of Projecto adopted the organization's core values of accuracy, dependability and trust and equipped him with the technical and behavioral attributes needed to deliver his role as master intermediary in a complex organization.

What was particularly telling about this rendering of the corporate brand in human form as applied to the project manager's role was his seemingly throw-away comments about "motivating people through force," the ability to deliver and "take punishment" and the need to see through a fog of apparent "nonsense."

These observations led onto a broader conversation about barriers to employee engagement as Projecto's colleagues started to reinforce some of the themes of power and hierarchy in the conception of their own brand champions and the stories they told.

As a result of the discussions that resulted, the organization's head of employee communication was able to make some significant changes to their feedback mechanisms. The organization was also able to make some very telling alterations to the way the brand refresh process was being communicated and to radically rethink a major employee engagement event to allow for much more active involvement of participants at all levels. The superheroes had achieved their mission and the brand would become the better for it.

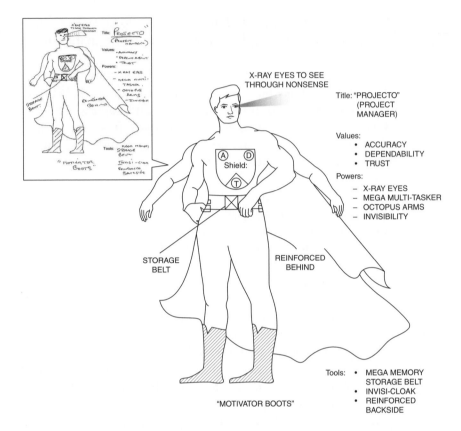

FIGURE 14   **Another example of a brand superhero – Projecto**

On a select number of occasions we've been asked to combine the brand superhero process with the creation of change management scenario based role-playing games where participants gather their brand superheroes and explore the challenges, opportunities and threats implied by major organizational change. Again, the Hero's Journey is a very useful tool if the challenge is a sequential, milestone based team task.

But it's by no means the only approach. Business simulation exercises which encourage teambuilding and innovation from a semi-fictitious safe space are hugely engaging and yield significant bottom line enhancing returns.

It's enlightening, not to mention great fun, to see people identifying and then inventing solutions to the usual threats they

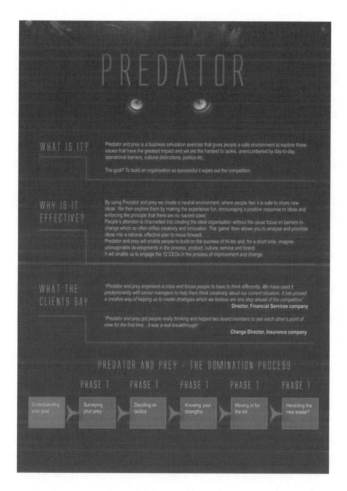

FIGURE 15 **Predator or Prey single page outline, a team based business simulation exercise designed to test the inventiveness of brand champions**

encounter in change scenarios based on past experience and the power of group thinking. Having the ability and freedom to invent superpowers and weapons to champion change in the best interests of promoting the brand may sound like so much "pie in the sky" but it's an engaging and empowering and ultimately useful involvement technique.

Paper based brand superheroes are liberating and educational and can be energizing. But at the end of the day, there's nothing like the real thing.

WHEN AND WHY HIGHLIGHT BRAND CHAMPIONS?

If you accept the authenticity argument, then you will appreciate that the business of seeking out and differentiating your heroes and brand champions is a sensitive one. You clearly want to highlight, reinforce and reward positive behavior. But you really don't want to alienate the uninvolved.

You also don't want to prejudice and embarrass those in the spotlight, as can often happen if the current culture is lagging behind the ideal. So how do you do it?

Put simply, there are a number of reasons for highlighting your champions:

- to illustrate what good looks like
- to reinforce the fact that the majority of brand management is behavioral and is therefore within the remit and the discretion of individuals (anyone can do it)
- to set an appreciative rather than critical tone
- to show that it benefits everyone not just the organization
- to tap into the powerful narrative traditions associated with the hero or champion drawn from mainstream society

Consider the growing trend for Meet the Team pages on company websites, for example. You know what I'm talking about: those sometimes amusing, sometimes informative, sometimes funky and often times cringe-worthy pen portraits of employees, "our people," meant to convey the employer brand personified. Whether actual photographs and mini biogs, camp, chromatic or animations, they say an awful lot about the corporate culture. They can be very effective. But nothing speaks louder than an incomplete gallery or a gang that's "too cool for school."

I don't believe in the notion that brand champions are some sort of internal marketing special forces unit tasked with recruiting their colleagues. I believe that organizations should strive to create an internal culture in which all employees become champions of the brand. This requires a comprehensive brand development strategy constructed through collaboration between Marketing and HR. A legitimate part of that strategy is to engage change agents to act as role models and help facilitate change, but the aim must be to facilitate a culture where it becomes cool to champion the brand.

An organization which has embraced all of these principles throughout its history, which consistently puts customers and employees first and is authentic in its depiction of its brand recently (2006) became the UK's most trusted retailer.

Research from the international institute AccountAbility and the National Consumer Council shows that The Co-operative is the most trusted brand in the eyes of UK consumers. In these dark days for many brands that's quite an achievement, especially as they beat off competition from the likes of mega brands such as Marks & Spencer, The Body Shop, John Lewis and Tesco. So how did they do it?

A LEGACY OF BRAND CHAMPIONS – THE CO-OP FINANCIAL SERVICES

The **co-operative** financial services
good with money

As we've explored, financial services brands are under siege like never before as the gap between espoused brand values and the reality experienced by staff and customers seemingly widens daily.

The media has been obsessed with the downfall of high-profile leaders but this brand disaster has deep roots. Or to put it another way, we may know who the rats are, especially in the city rat race... but the real problem lies with the fleas.

I was in the City, London's financial district, for a meeting the other day and found myself in Pudding Lane, infamous for being the source of the great fire of London. The fire has been heralded by historians as both the most tragic event to have befallen London and, ironically, its savior.

This isn't as paradoxical a statement as you might think. At the time of the fire, London had been in the grip of another epic threat, namely the plague or black death. It's a common misconception that this cataclysmic malaise was caused by rats. In truth it wasn't the rats, but the fleas which lived on them which caused the spread of the infection. Ironically, it wasn't until the great fire that the city was purged of the disease.

Understandably the financial districts are currently being targeted by the worldwide press as the source of the economic plague that has infected world markets. Indeed the high-profile figureheads, the directors of a select number of the mega brands within those financial districts, are being demonized for seemingly single-handedly bringing about the collapse of their institutions and, indeed, spreading this economic disease to related markets and economies.

This is where history and imagination collide. Brands aren't made overnight; cultures don't develop overnight, and unless there's an exceptional, one-off catastrophe, brands and the cultures that support them don't implode overnight.

The iniquity of the directors themselves and the problems the City faces are just the symptoms of a much more invidious infection. The disease of selfishness, short termism and winning at all costs has become an epidemic within this sector which has arguably spread into the nooks and crannies of world commerce. Simply getting rid of the directors isn't going to cure the problem, as we've seen since their balance sheets, propped up by public money, have started to recover.

The risk we currently face is that if we focus exclusively on the senior leaders, we forget that the malaise has already spread and infected the culture of the kingdoms they once ruled. Employee engagement and satisfaction figures in single digits, as I'm increasingly seeing at some formerly leading FS brands, are going to take as much repairing as their customer relations. These brands are dying from the inside and the worry is whether the management cadre appreciates that the antidote is in their hands.

Regulation won't solve the problem unless the regulators start to focus on the enabling activity that drives the brands rather than taxing the profits that stem from them. Regardless of short-term actions, unless leaders can start to:

- reinvent HR and get a grip on current vs. required culture
- proactively manage brands from the inside out rather than proliferating corporate and employer brands as two virtually disconnected initiatives
- professionalize internal communications
- respect and prioritize organization development
- focus on the development of line managers (ceos) as a priority
- forge more effective relationships between the external manifestation of brand and the link to the organization's values and the employees who keep the promises

the epidemic will doubtless surface again.

The renaissance of the mighty mutuals.

Set against this backdrop of imploding brands, many of the mutual societies, including the building societies in the UK, have experienced something of a renaissance. Ironically, there appears to be a newfound respect for classic, heritage brands in these dark days.

There was a time, not so very long ago, when the mutual societies were seen as deeply unfashionable and treated with the same disdain as a flat cap at Royal Ascot or white socks worn under a dress suit.

In *Brand Engagement*, I showcased Yorkshire Building Society for being true to its roots and focusing on employee engagement and brand building rather than selling out to the banking bandwagon. In light of what has happened to the banking sector, the YBS directors are pleased they stayed true to their roots.

Building societies emerged in the nineteenth century in England as financial mutual help organizations for workers who had been uprooted from village communities. They offered a way for workers to pool resources and fund and build their own housing in spite of the sometimes scandalous and always difficult economic conditions of the new cities.

Mutual societies, of which the Yorkshire Building Society and Nationwide are examples, as is The Co-operative and its financial services entity, The Co-operative Financial Services (CFS), can trace their roots back a couple of hundred years and several generations. Unlike most financial services organizations, they are run, ultimately, for the benefit of members rather than shareholders and take their foundation values very seriously. In fact, it can be argued that by insisting on values based leadership they were practicing holistic brand management long before the notion of brand management was given a catchy title.

To this day they are one of the few types of organizations where several generations of the same family are happy to still work hand in hand. Because of their founding values they have very loyal customers, suppliers and staff.

While their competitors resort to lawyers and due process to defend their much depleted positions from the wolf packs at the gate, which sadly includes a growing mob of disgruntled employees who are increasingly joining with shareholders baying for the blood of their respective boards, Nationwide has announced further expansion plans, CFS and Britannia have now merged, providing a much larger entity, and many mutuals are experiencing a flood of deposits and new accounts.

Cynics may claim that this simply represents a triumph of inertia over innovation and, yes, it's true that the mutuals have taken care with depositors' money, but they have also been significant innovators in their own right, especially on the employee brand engagement front.

The Co-operative Financial Services – Good with Money

The Co-operative is a major UK business and brand. Did you know that there are still more Co-operative outlets than McDonald's stores in the UK?

Perhaps you were aware that The Co-operative literally wears its corporate social responsibility credentials on its corporate sleeve and that one of The Co-operative's head offices in Manchester (the CIS Tower) is Europe's largest vertical solar project, with all three sides of its 25 stories clad in energy-generating solar panels.

FIGURE 16   **One of the many "totemic" Good with Money collaborative art installations created by employees**

The solar tower provides enough electricity to power 1000 PCs for a year.

The Co-operative Financial Services is part of The Co-operative Group, which is the world's largest consumer co-operative, with around five million members, over £14bn turnover and core business interests in financial services, food, travel, pharmacy and funeral care. The Co-operative Group has over 5000 retail trading outlets.

Following the merger with Britannia Building Society on August 1, 2009, the new organization is one of the largest and most diversified mutual businesses operating in both retail and corporate markets.

As part of The Co-operative Group, the new business is characterized by its unique ethical and member reward policies and very high levels of customer advocacy.

The combined business has £70bn in assets, 12,000 staff and nine million customers. It has over 300 high street branches, 20 corporate banking centers and a major presence in Manchester, London, Leek, Bristol, Plymouth, Skelmersdale and Stockport.

It is the only mutual organization that enables its members to earn financial rewards for the products they hold, as well as giving them the opportunity to have a say in how the business is run.

The Co-operative Group's financial services brands include The Co-operative Bank, The Co-operative Insurance, The Co-operative Investments, smile, the UK's first full internet bank, as well as Britannia and the group is one of the most significant investors in employer branding and brand engagement across sectors. Its state-of-the-art brand engagement experience has regularly attracted international visitors desperate to transfer best practices into their own organizations.

Under the "Good with Money" brand, in 2008 CFS invested heavily in brand building, as part of the wider group re-branding program, at a time when other organizations were cutting so-called discretionary spend. It has created and sustained a groundswell of brand engagement at all levels within the organization. Less concerned about featuring in world brand polls, CFS is passionate about colleague engagement, authenticity and remaining true to its founding values and principles.

In 2008 they devoted the best part of a floor at their Manchester HQ to a dynamic Good with Money brand walkthrough experience which every employee has sampled, interacted with and developed.

Importantly, they have recruited 40 brand champions to act as role models, facilitators and guides. But they don't fit the usual pushy, frustrated am dram, extroverted stereotypes we might expect.

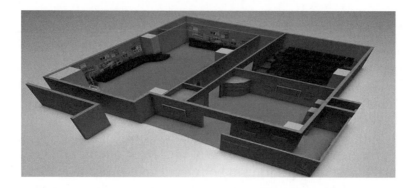

FIGURE 17   **A model of the Good with Money walkthrough experience at CFS HQ**

Mel's brand champion story

Melanie (Mel) Cartwright joined CFS as an analyst/programmer, having spent her early career at Bass, Marks & Spencer and British Aerospace. By her own admission she comes across as modest and personable, unused to public speaking. She certainly isn't the gushing, all teeth and talk "look at me" sort who would be expected to volunteer to facilitate large groups of up to 100. So she was perfect to be a CFS brand champion.

It was therefore something of a journey of discovery for Mel when she decided to put herself forward to play a leading part in the employee brand engagement program Good with Money. She realized that she would have to step out of her comfort zone and give presentations to a large audience from across the organization. Initially she found this a real challenge:

> *My first attempt at running a Good with Money group was terrifying. I am a manager but that meant nothing in this context. I felt exposed and nervous and unnatural representing our company to my colleagues. I also felt a great deal of responsibility to do the brand and the programme justice and reward people's faith in me.*

That's where Mel's own brand mentor, Rob Woolley, earned his corn.

Rob has the perfect brand ambassador's CV blending solid frontline experience with key brand-building executive roles. He was Director of The University for All at CFS and importantly had been Director of CFS Customer Services. Rob understood what customers value about the brand and what the real people who keep the brand alive relate to as he'd spent most of his career working shoulder to shoulder with them:

> *Mel was exactly what we wanted from a brand champion. She didn't upstage the participants, she cared deeply about our brand and wanted to transfer that enthusiasm to her colleagues. When we launched the Good with Money programme CFS wasn't exactly perceived as sexy or dynamic beyond these walls. In fact, within the business, we had started to believe that we were less than cutting edge ourselves. The whole purpose of the brand refresh was to re-assert our core values and regain pride in our brand against a backdrop of "bling" brands and their apparent attractions.*

It turns out that CFS was certainly right to focus on brand values given what subsequently happened to the sector. The leadership team recognized that brands are predominantly about behavior and, as a consequence, the engagement program was highly involving and group based and it has evolved over time.

FIGURE 18 **Photograph of the CFS Good with Money facilitators**

Brand ambassadors like Mel made great facilitators simply by being them-selves. We crafted an engaging brand experience but it's nothing without the conviction, credibility and authenticity that people like Mel bring. My job was to help the facilitators relax and be themselves. People like Mel are our brand.

Having met many of the Good with Money facilitators and having been escorted on the brand journey, the enthusiasm, camaraderie, pride and energy are infectious and it's interesting to note that I still have no idea where most of them sit in the CFS hierarchy.

I was thought to be a good facilitator because I'm honest and people could relate to me. By personalizing my talk further and taking a less formal and structured approach and introducing my own anecdotes it felt like I was telling real stories about real people. Suddenly I felt like I was being as on brand as I was encouraging my participants to be and I really started to relax and enjoy the sessions.

Part of the beauty of the CFS approach is that the facilitators didn't lecture the attendees but they brought the values to life through a series

FIGURE 19   **Photograph of participants creating a brand champion avatar**

of engaging, personalized and interactive experiences throughout the journey.

These sessions included a variation on the brand champion exercise in which participants create a succession of brand personalities which exemplify the brand values. They shared stories about how these brand personalities would walk, talk, act, look and feel and what they would believe.

The engagement experience had interactive presentations, competitions, dynamic "shows" and stimulating quizzes throughout, all of which were co-designed by the employees themselves.

In my time I've helped organizations develop interactive and engaging brand showcases and experiences. I've seen and developed events with higher production values, more glitz and drama, and even larger budgets but rarely something which has been as appropriate as the Good with Money experience or which has lasted as long.

The secret's in the people not just the process [says Rob]. *It is the behavior and culture that matters most and that's what remains embedded within the culture of the business once the events are over.*

FIGURE 20 **Attributes and behaviors of an "on brand" employee**

FIGURE 21   **Wall of brand champion pledges**

CFS subsequently received an award of excellence for internal events from the CiB British Association of Communicators in Business for the Good with Money event. But most importantly, their brand engagement initiative brought about lasting double-digit improvements in their employee engagement scores. As Richard Lewis, CFS Culture Manager, explains:

> *At CFS we measure colleague opinion on a range of subjects annually using our colleague opinion survey. We recognise that we cannot deliver our brand without the right behaviours, skills and levels of engagement among our people. We use the survey to measure our key vision measure of "market leading colleague satisfaction".*
>
> *Going forward, we will continue to develop ways to measure these vitally important aspects of our brand, as we further develop our people measurement strategy. We continue to look at our organisational culture and how it supports the delivery of the brand through our people.*

The Co-operative and CFS examples prove that the time has come to reconsider the humble mutual organizations (in the truest sense) who treasure their legacy and who position their values at the very

Question	2008 Fav	2007 Fav	Vs. 2007
Rating of CFS on being customer focused	81	57	+24
Rating of CFS on being a business that customers can trust	86	63	+23
The overall quality of service provided by CFS to customers	75	52	+23
Rating of CFS on being responsive to customer needs	68	47	+21
I would recommend CFS products and services to others	75	55	+20
Rating of CFS business prospects over the next two to three years	69	52	+17
I am proud to work for CFS	71	55	+16
My work and personal life are reasonably well balanced	71	55	+16
Management will use the information from this survey constructively	59	45	+14
I would recommend CFS to others as a place to work	62	49	+13
Rating of CFS as a place to work compared to other organizations	56	43	+13
Rating of CFS on departments working together to benefit the customer	44	32	+12
Rating of CFS on being innovative in developing new products or services	45	33	+12

FIGURE 22 **Impact of the CFS brand engagement program**

forefront of their brand. After all, what is a brand if it isn't about keeping the promises you make to your stakeholder communities regardless of whether your shareholders are independent or whether they include your colleagues, suppliers, customers and wider social community? What wouldn't shareholders, both internal and external, give for that kind of authenticity right now?

The evolving story of The Co-operative and CFS is a brand development legend which can trace its roots back hundreds of years. There's something very powerful about reflecting on a legacy and the confidence that comes from the fact that the brand has withstood countless challenges and has proven sustainability credentials. It's certainly inspirational for brand advocates like Mel and her colleagues, who are clearly the walking, talking embodiment of the brand even though they're too modest to allow me to afford them champion status. It's especially poignant and inspirational that people like Mel step forward every day, especially when times are as tough as they are for financial services brands in particular.

TOP CASE STUDY TIPS:

- organizations shouldn't blindly lust for Disney's magic dust when seeking employee brand engagement nirvana. It's better to develop something which reflects the current and desired culture
- the use of brand champions as facilitators of wider employee engagement is a tried and tested technique and preferable to external change agents as long as they are selected for and retain their authenticity
- lasting employee brand engagement can only be built in partnership with employees, not done to them
- brand champions exist at all levels
- measurement and evaluation is key to maintaining focus and motivation
- brand engagement efforts should focus on ALL of the 4Cs or stakeholder groups:
  - community
  - customers
  - colleagues
  - corporate

PART 4

EQUIPPING BRAND CHAMPIONS

BRAND DEVELOPMENT AND ENGAGEMENT DEVICES

We've already seen with the brand superhero exercise and the Co-operative case study that allowing people the space to experiment, to play and to innovate, trusting and truly empowering them, is an important aspect of any sense-making activity.

> *The biggest enemy to learning is the talking teacher.*
>
> John Holt

I've illustrated the difference between brand communication and internal brand engagement and, in Mel's story, demonstrated how

FIGURE 23 **Teaching effectiveness pyramid**
Source: California State University, Chico

deeply engaging it is for both facilitator and participants to be guided through a brand engagement experience by "one of your own." Involvement, discussion, exploration, practice and teaching others are all higher-order engagement techniques.

Having identifiable engagement leaders to role model the brand values and facilitate brand engagement experiences within their peer group is a tried and tested technique, provided they are encouraged and liberated to be authentic. There's also plenty you can do to equip your brand champions during their change journey, from skills development training through to providing them with a creative space and tools and techniques to encourage learning.

Part of the fun of developing a bespoke approach to brand engagement based upon the unique challenges faced by a particular organization is to co-develop the creative engagement interventions that are going to work for that particular group of people. It's important that these are not seen as the be all and end all of engagement as they so often are, or "silver bullet" solutions which will generate and sustain brand engagement in their own right. But they can be hugely influential and catalyzing signals of a sea change in the attitude of the organization toward employee brand engagement and will be very effective if they are:

- adopted by the internal change facilitators and not imposed by external catalysts
- complementary to the existing culture yet help to push back the boundaries
- clearly reinforcing the brand values
- clearly linked to tangible business outcomes

To the contrary, there's nothing worse than an engagement device or intervention that is out of synch with the context. Try using forum theater and actor-led role playing to encourage ideas generation, for example, after someone has just announced job cuts and see what response you get.

The options are endless but here's a select range of examples of the type of change interventions or engagement related "products" that have been used in these case studies or which brand change agents are likely to encounter in one shape or another:

- **The innovation hot house**
A permanent exhibit space in which the brand development journey can be mapped out from legacy through to vision. Creative tools and

inspirational spaces are ideally developed by employees, designed around the brand values, and teams can be scheduled to showcase "on brand" activity from their unit/division over a set period of time.

■ Values and behaviors academies

Aimed at first line managers (ceos), these are group development workshops designed around the brand values and aimed at personalizing, contextualizing and committing to the associated behaviors. They are a powerful way of connecting the brand to behavior based training and development and are particularly helpful for first line managers and leaders as they can be used to connect brand values to 360 degree assessment and the performance management process.

■ Brand champions X Factor

A one day event aimed at teasing out the hidden creative talents of employees competing to take control of the development of the next phase of the brand engagement journey, such as the next annual employee conference. Teams are tasked with pitching creative concepts based around the brand, adopting the medium of their choice as long as it reflects the brand values and the desired culture. A peer and panel voting system can be used to decide the outcome.

■ Predator or Prey business simulation exercise

Cross-functional teams explore the strengths and weaknesses of their existing brand in the context of a mythical new entrant to their market, launched by a team of their colleagues. Teams compete against each other using market intelligence to refine their brand in an attempt to achieve market dominance. A really engaging tool to develop teamwork, drive innovation and focus on the bottom line while role modeling core values and behaviors (see Figure 15 in Part 3).

■ Change roadmaps and the Hero's Journey

A large-scale board game connecting the storytelling and change management genres. During the game, brand superheroes embark upon a change journey of discovery and development aimed at bringing the brand to life and living the brand values. They recruit mentors and supporters on the way, encounter archetypes during the road of trials, and hopefully return with the brand elixir which will contain the secret for brand success.

■ **Artistic installations**

Collaborations between employees and ideally local artists to create regional artistic installations that embody and exemplify their brand values. These are then displayed throughout their network of offices (see Figure 16 in Part 3). Brand values given physical expression.

■ **Film school**

Creation of a mass documentary showcasing brand champions in action as ordinary members of staff go out into the community and film employees "doing things well." The aim is to deliberately catch people at their best and record appreciative comments from stakeholders and customers.

■ **Forum theater**

Using theater based techniques to develop customer service scenarios that encourage employees to understand and reconsider how the brand is perceived and then work together to rewrite the script to achieve the most favorable, on-brand outcomes. Alternatives have included using the conceits and structure of plays and opera to relaunch a brand, mission, strategy or vision.

■ **The live mobile experience**

Facilitated brand walkthroughs developed around the brand values and mounted on the back of a boat or an HGV. This is aimed at taking the brand walkthrough and sense-making exhibit to the people rather than expecting busy staff to drop everything to attend a conference.

■ **Permanent brand showcase**

An exhibit co-created by employees to chart the evolution of the brand which gives customer and employee insights through various media. This is probably one of the most common forms of brand showcase, offers itself to multimedia design and implementation, and is very useful for inducting new entrants. It is most powerful if combined with face-to-face facilitation (see Figure 17 in Part 3).

■ **Brand change roadmap or navmat**

An interactive tool created using electronic gaming technology, expanded to enable medium size team interaction and real time play beamed live to a large screen. Participants are set a series of brand-related tasks relevant to their own brand, values and behaviors and are invited to navigate a physical maze or journey linked to a computer and monitor setting out their progress against various change goals.

■ Virtual brand tour
Brand walkthrough experiences created in a virtual environment and usually hosted by an avatar or the actual online presence of a senior leader, and available on demand, online.

■ Brand maps
A static variant on the above which uses the thinking behind mind mapping to create a physical landscape, a picture in which the brand is placed in the context of the mission, vision, values and core elements of the strategy and change plan.

■ Stories and storytelling
Professional storytellers entertain and educate in equal measure, encouraging employees to share the myths and lore associated with their organization, brand and products. These stories can then be used as the basis for a brand storybook which evolves with each generation.

■ Brand eisteddfod
A brand engagement festival which plays on the ancient social instincts of co-creating oral lore. It usually features poetry and song during which teams interpret the evolution of their brand and the strategic context in ways that can be engaging, entertaining and memorable.

Here are a couple of examples of just how creative people like to be. The first was turned into a song by a group of retailer managers focused on the subject of corporate social responsibility, and the second was acted out by members of a telecommunications company as part of their brand relaunch.

When branding goes wrong

A torn bird's wing flaps wildly on the iron thornbush.
No body. No beak. No bits of bird.
Just wing and wind and point and barb.
White and red tarandula
Frantic spastic
Spasm of plastic bag

> *Cast aside*
> *To rustle in place of sparrow and thrush*
> *In fields turned high street made retail park*
> *A one-stop-shop for the perpetual motion*
> *Of persistent plastic people*
> *The brand misplaced*
> *Anger agitating the branded wound.*

Our A–Z of brand engagement

A   *"Anarchy in the UK." The Sex Pistols taught us a lesson about engagement and control that's worth remembering as we become part of the establishment ourselves. Let's not forget our roots when we become managers.*

B   *"Brand BS Bingo!" A great way to pass the time at the next leadership conference, and a way of checking if we've somehow become our own version of our worst managers and stopped being real.*

C   *Is for credibility. We lose it when we try to be something we aren't.*

D   *Enough planning already – just DO It!*

E   *Encourage your line managers to be the great communicators people already know them to be.*

F   *Facebook is the organization's friend. Social media isn't a fad, let's embrace it and stop trying to police it.*

G   *"It's great after being out late, walking my baby back home." Now that's engagement!*

H   *Hire people who are in tune with our brand values or it's going to be a lose/lose situation.*

I   *However well crafted communication should start and end with an "I" – "I see what's in it for me!"*

J   *Jack Johnson. He's on message with several generations! What can we learn from Mr. Cool?*

K   *Keeeeeeeeeeeeeep listening!*

L   *Leaders look in the mirror when things are going wrong. Like what you see?*

M   *Managers are an endangered species we're not campaigning to save.*

N   *"Naked" (and other "power" words).*

O   *Ordinary is good. Take back ordinary. Let's make authentic communication ordinary, the norm round here!*

P   *Planning is our friend. But rather like doughnuts, too much planning really slows you down.*

Q   *"The Queen is dead. Long Live the Queen." Whatever you may think of them our Hero Leaders come and go. Line managers last a lot longer.*

R   *"With great power comes great responsibility."*

S   *Supercalifragilisticexpialidocious. You remembered it. Geddit?*

T   *Taste, sight, sound, smell, touch – brand engagement's about appealing to the lot.*

U   *U2!?. More than a legendary rock band but a reminder that we've a great network out there and we've all got something to share and learn.*

V   *VALUES! Our brand is nothing unless we can all live our values! Repeat after us ...*

W   *WE is what's important, me, you and the customer.*

X   *Factor! After the re-brand it will also mark the spot!*

Y   *Aren't you engaged yet? Are you not entertained?*

Z   *Zoo! Whatever formal engagement strategies there may be it's always going to be a fantastic, colorful jungle out there.*

These are just a modest sample of the fun to be had when people have the freedom to develop their own ways of exploring and communicating the brand. The possibilities are as endless and as unique as the infinite combinations of the imaginations of the groups who generate them. But don't think for a moment that any of the above creative interventions were invented by junior staff or juveniles. The vast majority were co-created by senior managers and above who were grateful for the chance to throw away the PowerPoint decks and lecterns and throw off the "corporate officer" pretence for a few hours.

Brand engagement possibilities are boundless and the involvement process itself can be extremely engaging, enjoyable and memorable if designed and facilitated appropriately.

As popular as they are, and as tempting as it is to focus on them, these totemic interventions, however, mustn't be positioned as the be all and end all of your brand engagement drive. However creative the approach, however effective the facilitators and however interactive the sessions, they will eventually be dismissed and remembered as part of the litany of failed corporate catharsis unless they are employed as part of a wider strategy designed to permanently develop an internal culture that is based around, reinforces and sustains the brand values and on-brand behavior.

BRAND DEVELOPMENT AND STORYTELLING

I've talked at length about the power of storytelling before but you can't underestimate the relationship between employee engagement and the representation of the change process in terms and in a format people can relate to and understand. People respond to narrative; it's embedded in our cultural DNA. So why would we ignore it in the workplace, where (like it or not) we spend most of our lives?

If leadership is primarily about inspiring a group of individuals to come together for a common purpose and achieve something greater than the sum of their parts, then stories are essential to articulate what that could look like, that vision. Building brands means building stories about "what is and what can be."

Noel Tichy in his book *The Leadership Engine* remarks that:

The best way to get humans to venture into unknown terrain is to make that terrain familiar and desirable by taking them there first in their imagination.

When a leader, wherever they sit in the organization, inspires, they breathe life and energy into their followers. Reflecting on Churchill's extraordinary speeches, for example, it's clear that no amount of models or funky graphics would have had the effect of his well-chosen, powerful words. Martin Luther King Jr. had a dream – he didn't have a change imperative or a brand goal. Obama told uplifting stories and made even the most cynical people feel positive and empowered with the chant "yes we can."

Getting people to do something differently or to do different things is tough. Change may be scary but there's nothing more terrifying than vagueness and uncertainty. We have an innate fear of the unknown, especially when we care about the people involved or even the organization and the brand in question.

I bet you can recall the strapline to the 1978 movie *Jaws II*: "Just when you thought it was safe to go back in the water." These few words tap into the legacy of the first film and the deep paranoia that resulted from Spielberg's creation, which led to reports of people even checking the swimming pool for a dorsal fin not once but twice before a dip, after they had seen the film. This strapline to the sequel creates an image (a threatening expanse of dark ocean), a sense (learned fear) and a feeling (a nasty one).

Compare these words with "critical inflection point" and "dedicated brand capability" – nonsensory words that dominate most corporate communication. If you assemble enough of these nonsensory words in one place you create a vacuum and you trip a switch in the listener's brain, the lights go out and they start thinking about something else. These words are part of the impersonal vocabulary which people use when they're trying to sound clever or scientific and to conceal their true emotions.

We've created a myth in corporate communication that we can't be reassured by feelings in business and that the language of emotions is the language of metaphor. That it is somehow unseemly and should be confined to fiction.

But there's every chance you'll remember your first kiss, the first record you listened to on your Walkman, the feel of your baby's blanket, the smell of your grandmother's Sunday roast or the visual imagery associated with loved ones.

So, if you want to connect people with the values connected with your brand and the feeling you want your brand to instill in them, can you expect it to happen using statistics and yield charts? People need the metaphor, comparisons, similes, sensations that evoke feelings. They need heroes they can relate to, situations and context, stories and best of all they need to experience the brand for themselves. But how?

As a literary genre of high culture, romance or chivalric romance refers to a style of heroic prose and verse narrative that has been passed through to us from aristocratic literature of Medieval and Early Modern Europe. Chivalric romance narrates fantastic stories about the marvelous adventures of a chivalrous, heroic knight who embarks on a quest during which he and subsequently the culture he represents are transformed forever. Isn't that a lot more exciting than SWOT or PEST analysis in pursuit of a change imperative?

Popular literature contains ironic, satiric or burlesque intent, just as romances often rework legends and fairy tales like traditional stories about heroes and champions from Charlemagne, Beowulf and Roland to King Arthur. These legends underpin most written and visual drama from business books to bedtime stories. So why aren't they used in everyday business communication?

As I indicated when describing Campbell's analysis of cross-cultural mythology and the Hero's Journey, the romantic tradition can provide powerful clues about how to forge closer relations between employees and their brands. There may well be some modern audiences who don't recognize the protagonists but they will certainly recognize the narrative structures, beats and key themes. So why wouldn't you incorporate these storytelling devices into the mythology surrounding the evolution of your brand? Why, then, is every product launch positioned as if it is a brand new story rather than part of a heroic brand adventure? Regardless of whether it's arrogance associated with the vanity of a new campaign, insecurity about potential comparisons with the classic motifs or simply failure to appreciate what has gone before, it is counter-productive to ignore the legacy of stories from which the brand is comprised.

Throughout the romantic tradition of storytelling there is a marked tendency to emphasize themes of courtly love, such as faithfulness in adversity, and other moral codes and themes which help to create value sets upon which a society is dependent. All a bit too emotional for corporation speak?

If we're mature enough to appreciate that the telling of stories and conveying of lore is an essential part of human cultural behavior, regardless of country of origin, we should be able to appreciate the power of values inspired storytelling as a brand-building discipline. Stories have a genuine place in business. Brand champions certainly use stories to generate advocacy and pride.

Alan Clarke at the Northern Ireland Tourist Board spoke passionately about the link between their corporate re-brand, his childhood and the future of the country during his emotional and heartfelt keynote address to his employees. He had the courage to be vulnerable, to step out from behind the lectern, and refused to batter his colleagues with the blunt instrument of PowerPoint graphs or Mori polls proving the need for change in his country.

One of the most persistent criticisms I hear of brand refresh or redevelopment exercises and related change programs is the relentless focus on the future without acknowledgment of the legacy of the brand. This blinkered approach demotivates, disrespects and disenfranchises the people who built the brand and who mostly still work there. It leaves people feeling stressed and incomplete as only looking forward flies in the face of the rules of narrative.

These initiatives often appear to come from nowhere and are often criticized as being the pet projects of agency-tied marketing directors as a result. When the brand is positioned as the property of the Marketing department alone, you have a very real problem which no amount of advertising spend can cure.

Storytelling provides a fertile ground:

- for bridging the past and the vision, for providing context
- for introducing brand values in the light of corporate social responsibility
- for making the most of and protecting the people who work within the organization and championing the customer's cause

These are all themes with which people can connect, which elicit an emotional and engaging response. These themes exist in the everyday narrative of the business whether the leaders acknowledge them or not, so why not make the most of that connection and resulting energy and use it to bring about change?

Many medieval romances recount the marvelous adventures of a chivalrous, heroic knight, often of superhuman ability, who, abiding by chivalry's strict codes of honor and demeanor, goes on a quest and fights and defeats monsters and giants, thereby winning favor with a lady and his community. As we've seen when exploring the Hero's Journey, business leaders are unconsciously judged by similar criteria.

What a pretext this provides for a CEO presentation or brand champions orientation briefing. Isn't an invitation to join a senior leader on a journey of adventure and exploration more exciting than a "change imperative" and restructure? Isn't it a better alternative than "frightening the horses" by impressing upon people dry responsibilities and objectives as they attempt, often for the first time, to come to terms with an emotionally charged change or don their game faces and facilitate brand engagement sessions in front of their peers?

When I'm asked to help develop brand engagement events (what I call totemic engagement activities – reflecting the importance organizations often place on them), I'm a big fan of selecting brand champions and facilitators from the junior ranks.

Whether it's to interview the chairman on stage, compere a conference or run a brainstorm, asking junior or more circumspect potential champions to step forward earns instant respect from their colleagues and raises the participation bar significantly. People love the underdog; it plays to notions of heroism, and people will remember the dynamic as a key moment in the change journey long after the words have faded.

An organization which has taken all of the above into account is the Northern Ireland Tourist Board, long-time brand development underdogs yet recent winners of a prestigious CIB marketing award following their major, inside and out brand refresh.

REINVENTING THE STORY OF NORTHERN IRELAND

Mention Northern Ireland and most people instantly think of civil unrest, mistrust and factional fighting. Ironically, however, people also associate the Irish with friendliness, humor, the gift of the gab, storytelling and a rich heritage of myths and legends.

The latter characteristics had been frustrated until recently in the North, where stories had sadly but understandably become fixated on the "troubles." There can be few more challenging brand reinventions than the one the Northern Ireland Tourist Board embarked upon when they sought to permanently change the way people thought of their brand and the stories they told as a result.

FIGURE 24   Brochure advertising the Antrim storytelling experience

Northern Ireland is currently experiencing an unprecedented tourism renaissance as, following the eventual success of the peace process, more and more people from around the world are gradually finding the confidence to explore this beautiful and innately hospitable country. As a result the network of Tourist Information Officers (TIOs) situated in Tourist Information Centres (TICs) across the country have found themselves very much in demand. They consequently needed to find new and fresh ways to connect customers with local attractions and unique delights. One of the approaches they have started to adopt is to confidently connect their legacy to their future and to start telling stories again.

The advertising campaign that supported the Northern Ireland re-brand emphasizes the journeys of discovery visitors make as they explore the country and learn for the first time that St. Patrick is actually buried there, for example, or discover the fine produce or stumble upon caves reputed to contain mermaids or upon surf beaches and bike trails of mythical proportions. The stories become self-perpetuating and lead to the creation of even more legends to be re-told by a growing band of internal and external brand advocates.

The advertising was a product of confidence and forward thinking, a sense that the time had come for the Tourist Board to respond to the changing priorities of the Northern Ireland government and commit to a range of key performance indicators based around attracting visitors to the country and making their visit enjoyable, memorable and an addition to the cache of stories. NITB needed to generate substantial returns for a major capital investment in tourism.

As Gillian Magee (Senior Manager, Marketing, Strategy and Brand) explains:

We knew we had to reinvent the way people saw Northern Ireland as well as the way we managed tourism. We had to redevelop the brand and bring it to life. Northern Ireland Tourism needed a framework to keep the promise ie:

- *Build the product*
- *Develop a quality experience*
- *Promote the destination*

We had to develop a brand for everyone involved in Northern Ireland tourism and engaged with 1000 stakeholders to develop a shared vision which had to be owned by all.

It is difficult for people to get to grips with "branding." It's one of those buzz disciplines that needs examples, stories, to be linked to outputs that illustrate the brave new world and new way of working.

As an organization we were very clear about "What we needed to do" but we needed to revisit "How it should be done" to best effect. As brand champions it was up to us to make "branding" tangible for the industry to give them ideas so that they could improve "HOW" they deliver visitor experiences.

We undertook a substantial visitor attitude survey and identified the areas of the visitor journey that required attention. We developed pilot projects to improve each of these "shortcomings" all along the customer journey and worked with a series of partners to deliver them, to change the outcome of the stories visitors tell.

As Gillian points out, some people still struggle with the word "brand." But they understand reputation.

Integral to the NITB brand development journey is the need to enable tourists to experience what they evocatively call their "awakening" and to "uncover" their stories and in the process reinvent the reputation of the region. Their approach is both mysterious and tantalizing, like being involved in a treasure hunt and hopefully uncovering a hidden gem. And it's working well.

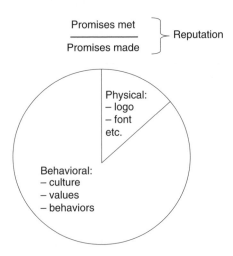

FIGURE 25 **What is a brand?**

FIGURE 26   **The core brand partnership**

The NITB directors had the foresight to appreciate that advertising and refreshing the customer-facing brand wouldn't be enough. Relatively early on in the process they bought into the need for a joined-up approach to brand management with the internal and external facing parts of the business working hand in hand and the executive team as a whole role modeling the brand values.

While redeveloping the Northern Ireland tourism brand, the Tourist Board executive team has simultaneously been refreshing their own organization brand. They have also adopted a deliberately emotional element within the NITB corporate brand values by choosing *respect* as one of only three cornerstone values. They are determined to practice what they preach both within and beyond the corporate HQ, recognizing how important it is to uncover and promote brand champions throughout their network of positive influence.

The work with the Tourist Information Centres was one of 20 brand development pilot projects, but a very important one. In the context of a conference repositioning the Northern Ireland brand, in order to rebuild the confidence of the TIOs, battered by decades of negativity, they encouraged these dedicated brand ambassadors to start to regain

Champions of the Northern Ireland tourism experience

OUR MISSION

To get Northern Ireland on everyone's wish list by:

- Helping Northern Ireland confidently move on
- Co-creating the new Northern Ireland experience
- Enabling tourists to experience our awakening and uncover our stories

Our Values

Respect	Teamwork	Expertise
Listening	Inclusive	Confident
Adapting	Supportive	Useful
Acting with Integrity	Together	Innovative
Personable	Unified	Brave
Responsive	Empowering	Knowledgeable
"Treating others as we would like them to treat us."	"Working with and not against others."	"Applying what we know for mutual benefit."

FIGURE 27   **The NITB behavioral brand framework – vision, mission and values**

a sense of perspective and appreciate how good they and their bounty of wares actually are. With a simple exercise called:

My Story
Your Story
Our Story

the TIOs were encouraged to tell each other:

- why they joined
- achievements they were proud of
- stories that hinted at their values

Gradually these stories were connected to the fresh Northern Ireland brand and associated values, the vision and mission until the collective penny dropped. These brand ambassadors, however, weren't really being asked to be anything other than themselves.

It felt a little awkward at first, but eventually the TIOs committed to the notion that uncovering and capturing the stories relating to their local areas could potentially give them a real unique selling proposition to be proud of. In the process they were serving a cause very close to their hearts and helping the country move confidently ahead.

First there were the myths and legends of Northern Irish lore to be rediscovered, the stuff about ghosts, highwaymen, romantic poets and wandering minstrels that the visitors from abroad in particular love.

The myths then became linked to certain notable sites and eventually tours and schedules started to emerge:

1.54   Arrive Creggan Church and Graveyard

Creggan Visitor Centre is in the grounds of the local Church of Ireland church which houses a permanent exhibition on the poets and people of Creggan. The historical graveyard is the burial place of the three 18th century Gaelic poets: Art Mac Cumhaigh, Padraigh Mac Ghiolla Fhiondain and Seamus Mor Mac Murphy (the latter being both poet and notorious outlaw)...The O Neill Vault (1480–1820)...contains over seventy skulls...the family went into exile after the 1641 rebellion failed.

In an extension of the My Northern Ireland storytelling initiative, a local initiative spearheaded by Brenda Murphy, Visitor Information Manager, included a competition now run annually which identifies the most inspiring tours, gives publicity and recognition to the local brand champions, and shares best practices widely. There's no gold star or gong for the winning TIC. Instead, the competition winner gets to host their colleagues for a day as part of a recognition package:

Our aim is first to share the stories amongst the TIO community and then to capture and collect the stories, to compile a storybook that evolves over time, to share best practices but importantly to create a sense of community amongst the brand ambassadors. It's really starting to bring the brand to life where it counts.

Brenda Murphy

4pm Bus departs for tour of Limavady Workhouse for tales and ghostly encounters.

5pm Group board bus and depart for Dungiven Priory where they will meet the ghosts of Finvola O'Cahan, her lover Angus McDonnell and hear the haunting cry of the banshee, Grainne Rua and a musical rendition of the "Finvola, Gem of the Roe."

5.45pm Depart for Windyhill Road to the site of the "murderhole" where Cushy Glen, the notorious highwayman, buried his victims. Prepare for blood thirsty tales.

Back at NITB HQ, they have embarked upon a comprehensive overhaul of the NITB brand and are well down the track of a complementary culture change program designed to ensure that everyone really "lives the brand." Given years of negativity and the uphill struggle they've had promoting Northern Ireland, the NITB team

FIGURE 28   **Photograph of NITB Tourist Information Officers during a local storytelling tour**

has been overwhelmingly enthusiastic and has embraced change in the main. But as Gillian states, *"the successful transformation of the culture will be key to sustaining the bold promises made during the brand refresh."*

The brand development change program has included:

- understanding and modeling the current culture as well as desired future culture needed to bring the brand to life
- comprehensively refreshing the physical elements of the NITB brand
- redeveloping and simplifying the values set and associated behaviors
- values and behaviors workshops for all line managers (ceos)
- major redesign of the internal space to reflect the values
- redevelopment of all people processes, including training and development and performance management, to align with the brand values
- an articulation of the NITB story accompanied by a change roadmap
- workshops with the senior leadership team to ensure they individually and collectively walk the talk

FIGURE 29 **NITB employees working together at the first brand engagement event**

- a brand ambassador recognition and best practice sharing program
- a line management development program
- a professional internal communication program including engagement events, now designed and developed by the employees themselves using the brand values as guiding principles

With the possible exception of the re-branding of Johannesburg in South Africa, I don't think I've been involved with a brand development program which is so emotive, calls so much for respecting but overcoming the past, and which is so dependent upon sociopolitical factors beyond the control of the brand managers. But the brand champions at NITB, which for me now includes the vast majority of the employees, and the wider network of TIOs have to be admired for their enthusiasm, passion and tenacity.

They still have significant challenges and the journey is ongoing. Doubtless there will be setbacks along the way and it's certainly going to be hugely important that the senior team walk the talk, but the emerging story of the redevelopment of the NITB and Northern Ireland brand is a compelling tale of how to build a network of brand superheroes within the corporate HQ and wider network of representatives. What better brand development cause can you be involved with than one which helps decide the fate of your country? And what better way of role modeling your national brand than by bringing it to life from the inside?

FIGURE 30 **Picture of NITB staff at the Staff Conference. Living the brand is all about bringing the NITB values to life**

> ## TOP CASE STUDY TIPS:
>
> - don't spend money on advertising unless you can first back up your promises
> - culture change and brand development need to go hand in hand
> - values and behaviors need to be hardwired into key people processes like performance management and communication
> - employee involvement and engagement unleashes confidence in your brand champions
> - the story of the brand evolves over time and your brand stories can be a powerful mark of uniqueness if you use them well
> - if culture change is to be sustained, leaders have to be role models

STORIES FROM THE "MAGNIFICENT SEVEN"

If the brand reigns supreme then undoubtedly the working heroes in the corporate kingdom are the brand champions who uphold the brand values and cultural code. But as we've already observed, they aren't always obvious and don't always come with gaudy heraldry and noisy fanfare.

Over the course of the past few years I've interviewed a select group of these brand champions from world-class brands, both together and individually, in an attempt to get to the core of what makes the typical brand champion tick. They are drawn from diverse organizations that are highly respected for brand management:

- Manchester United Football Club
- Google
- Virgin
- McDonald's
- John Lewis
- Oxfam
- First Direct

During our time together I asked them a series of questions relating to ten key themes outlined in *Brand Engagement* as being critical success factors on which holistic brand management depends.

The individuals range from a senior executive through to a junior customer service operative. I have chosen not to identify the individuals, for the sake of practicality, to encourage openness but also to ensure that it's what they say rather than who they are that counts. The aim is to attempt to highlight general best practices rather than focus on any one particular organization. You'll doubtless have fun trying to guess who's who. What follows is a flavor of the highlights of our discussions.

1. *To what extent would you agree that it's the **chief engagement officers**, the workaday everymen within organizations, who are primarily responsible for internal brand engagement (more ceo and less CEO)?*

C – "Undoubtedly our CEO is the figurehead of our business and is seen by everyone inside and outside of the business as the embodiment of our brand. But we're fairly unique I guess. There's still a feeling here that we're somehow a group of small, intimate, entrepreneurial, empowered teams despite the fact we now work for a mega brand. There's a strong sense of fun which does come from the top and for the overwhelmingly most part, we're definitely proud of our brand, will happily talk about the brand in a social setting and this pride carries through into the way we work."

D – "Our brand is all about offering a personal service in a market that's becoming increasingly depersonalized and automated. You can't do that without everyone buying into the values and working style that makes us different. We spend a lot of time and effort emphasizing this point from recruitment, through induction and onto performance management. This makes line managers vitally important to sustaining the brand."

A – "Arguably our brand is so 'out there' that people are usually making a value judgment first and foremost when they choose to join us. Working here is more of a vocation than a job. Brand engagement is everyone's responsibility."

E – "Being 'on brand' here isn't an option it's what you sign up to when you join. This is reinforced through tried and tested processes that are appropriate for our business. They include input from team members to recruitment and retention of staff. The buck stops with the branch management. But there's a strong emphasis on individual accountability which is reinforced through tried and tested recognition systems."

G – "We operate to a partnership ethos which clearly communicates the fact that we all represent the brand in our interactions with customers as well as with each other. Line managers are important but we're all ceos, to use your term, and peer pressure through example is what motivates us the most."

B – "We're all supposed to be ceos here, communication is a core competency. We're all supposed to be brand champions as well and in the main we are. You don't really hear cynicism here; griping about pressure, yes; whinging about factors beyond our control sometimes, but people are proud to work here and this is reflected in our employee surveys and in the feel of the place."

2. *The brand doesn't reside in the Marketing department. It isn't distinct from the organization. It is the organization; it's the sum of the **promises made less promises kept**. Does that hold true where you work?*

B – "Our brand is known throughout the world. It's largely a tribal thing, you either love it or if you're not in the tribe you probably don't. But chances are you at least respect it. That's the power of a strong and dominant brand. The influence of our marketing department is immense. But if we don't deliver on the front line we all suffer."

E – "It's the same here. The difference is that attention to detail is critical. The slightest slip by the most junior member of staff can undermine the brand, affect the franchise, and cost jobs. We have to keep the promises made by our immense marketing machine. We wouldn't have the brand without powerful marketing. But without our people there would be no one to deliver the brand. It's a powerful combination when we get it right. We have our detractors, that's for sure. Given our global domination though you have to say that we get it right most of the time. We talk about brand all the time but about the way we need to act to bring it to life for customers time and again."

C – "That's a hell of a lot of pressure to have to work under. Sure we have processes that are very, very important. We don't just deal in promises but people do sometimes trust us with their lives. It doesn't feel that scary though. It's important for people to relax and enjoy themselves as it brings the best out of them. Our brand promises are about the good things in life and we still have a fresh and innovative outlook. But living up to those promises doesn't feel like a chore. We talk about brand here whenever we talk about strategy. It's part of the way we work."

A – "Brand and brand values need to be practical but inspirational as well. Organizations should appeal to people's morals as much as the run of the mill stuff. It helps to connect with customers as well as staff and gives us all something to live up to if it's going to be more than hot air."

D – "We harness information to provide a personalized service based on customer needs rather than pushing products. Our brand relies on correctly identifying and meeting those needs. So we have to ensure that both our services and products have the range and quality to meet those needs. We monitor all key aspects of employee and customer satisfaction. Where the two meet is where the brand magic happens I guess."

F – "One of the things that's most important to remember is that we're all customers first and foremost – we use our services daily. We always try and keep that mentality, that perspective alive. We respect what we have and don't change things for the sake of it but in a very competitive and changing market we need challenge and fresh insights. We work hard to create a positive but critical environment even though that sounds a bit more stern than it actually is in practice."

B – "It's the same here. Most of us are dedicated fans first and foremost."

G – "Customers come to us because of our reputation for providing a quality service and product. By doing that consistently, price is not usually an issue although we have that covered as well with a price beating pledge. Yes, things like the quality of the products and the promise-making can be centrally controlled. But customers most remember the manner of the staff they meet. I'm confident the vast majority of my colleagues would say the same."

3. *To manage the brand effectively, it's essential to have a close working relationship between the triumvirate of **CEO's office, Marketing and HR**, traditionally the custodians of the internal and external promise-making parts of the business. Do you see that happening?*

G – "Again, we're very much a partnership based upon the founding ideals of our forefathers and this carries through into the way we work. To some extent we're encouraged to have a departmental mentality, to be great at our specialism. But this isn't a business where there's much buck passing and I believe that comes right from the top."

A – "We try to operate a flat, nonhierarchical structure with backwards and forwards dialog. It's fairly unique in my experience in that we work across functions and it's the least 'departmentalized' environment I've worked in. The brand and our beliefs absolutely influence the way all of us work and we all feel like advocates. We all still talk about the time we sent a delegation of staff to the AGM of a pharmaceutical company having made them minor share holders. These ambassadors, not our CEO, lobbied the board about the pricing policy. I guess that shows how responsibility for the brand is lived out live."

D – "The credit crunch and resulting recession has created some very challenging conditions for us. However, rather than hide behind the Boardroom door, our CEO and top team held a series of 'direction' sessions attended by all of our several thousand staff. Even though many of the messages were difficult, understanding and commitment levels following these sessions were still measured in the 90% plus bracket. This gives an important insight into how our brand is managed and maintained internally."

B – "The brand is everything here from the suppliers we select (who need to share our values) through to the staff we select and the way we market to our customers, who have an intimate connection to the brand worldwide. I guess that can't happen without close partnership but the influence of the marketing department is immense."

E – "Our process management approach really is the stuff of legend and applies to the way we manage our marketing as much as the way we manage our people and our reputation. The brand is at the heart of everything rather than any department and the CEO is less relevant to most staff than their line manager, who really has to embody the brand values and leadership style every day."

F – "My company's name was one of the first words my young daughter (unprompted) learned to spell. That sounds lame I know, but it's true. I'm immensely proud to work there.

It's fantastic on my CV. People love the brand both within and outside the business. People have a positive opinion of the brand

and it transfers to your sense of pride in your company. Goes to show if you just produce a good product it can translate into something remarkable (something worth remaking). I don't attribute this to any department, it's everywhere from the food and offices through to doing good things in the community; empowering people internally; providing learning opportunities; ensuring third-party suppliers respect the brand when working for us; recruiting great people; creating a real sense of energy and passion; getting the small things right and projecting an image to employees of a company that cares. I guess that comes from the top team living our values first."

4. *Brand development activity needs to be expressed as part of an **ongoing narrative**, a story which respects the legacy of the brand and engages all stakeholders with the future. How does your organization capture this story?*

B – "We have a strong heritage and rich historic base that makes us different. But the story has had to evolve in line with the changing customer base. We cater to this by involving legendary former employees in the club's profile and management to retain the thread and by creating a family culture within the organization. People tell stories here about memorable moments from the past, link these to images and faces and names and pass these down just like the fans of our brand do when they bring their children and friends here."

C – "Oh we certainly share stories of exceptional customer service through our internal communication channels and we make a very big thing of capturing positive press and PR. It helps us to create a culture of 'us vs. them' in the press when we talk about our competitors and this contributes to teamwork internally. There's an annual staff garden party which includes our families, a great chance to share things face-to-face and create a sense of a wider community which loves this brand. We're all very aware that the story of our brand is still very much fresh and dynamic and is continuously evolving. It's motivating to feel part of that dynamism. I also know that many organizations don't seem to value things in the same way and are offloading many of their employee perks and benefits or assets just because they can get away with it."

D – "When I think of our story I have a very clear sense of where we came from, our context, and where we're going. The story isn't cluttered, largely because:

- our internal brand values are identical to our external brand values
- our CEO addresses us direct at least twice a year
- we have regular team briefing facilitated by line managers
- we all have a brand booklet
- measurement is clear and transparent
- communications groups meet to deal with any specific bottlenecks or issues

None of this is rocket science as such but it all contributes towards a clear sense of being part of an ongoing journey."

E – "The history of the brand is an integral part of induction. You have to be clear about that before you buy into your first set of objectives. We have very sophisticated internal communication from the center covering all channels but daily team briefings, face-to-face, are part of our culture."

A – "The story of our brand is the sum of the stories of our customers and the impact we're making. We make a point of ensuring that as many of our employees as possible visit projects throughout the world at some point, including administration staff. We have an annual Assembly weekend for representatives in which we cover a lot of the ground about where we're going, what we're achieving etc. and share best practices. Stories keep us going. Hierarchies don't get in the way here. Our philosophy is based on helping others help themselves and that applies inside our organization as well."

F – "This place is set up to ensure that people meet and talk all the time. The environment is fantastic and creates a real buzz around sharing ideas, concepts, and yes, stories. You would be amazed at the quality but modesty of the average Joe here. But the stories you'll gather about empowered people doing extraordinary things and very quickly making an impact is what really impresses me more than any big, grandstand events or high-profile storytelling. The narrative about the business is everywhere, we're living it in real time and it feels that way. It's a bit like a hive."

G – "We don't work in such a high-tech environment. Our focus is on providing classic service, which makes the reflection back to our roots an important source of stability and continuity. A lot of thought goes into any company-wide events, which are always couched in the context of our brand and our values. We're very conscious of our part in the story of our brand as a result and this is reinforced through the recruitment, appraisal, and development processes and the well thought through job perks that build commitment."

5. *The **vision, mission, values and behaviors** need to be reflected in the brand, and the brand management process should be an integral part of business strategy. How aware are you of the connection between this and the brand?*

D – "The links are made very clear during induction and reinforced through appraisals. The values come to the fore at appraisals. We also equip all employees with documentation about the brand, mission, and values. This is not an organization where colleagues don't recognize the organization in the adverts."

E – "It's exactly the same here. We do a lot more product and campaign advertising but we're briefed well in advance and the core values always remain the same. The wider business strategy isn't as relevant as the local plan and we make sure our people are aware of what that is and how they fit in."

A – "People don't get to work here if they just want a job. With so many volunteers we're not in this for the money. So the vision, mission, and values are absolutely at the core of our brand. We're still in a competitive sector challenging for market share but our difference is reflected in our brand and the link to the vision etc. I often think other organizations can learn a lot about authenticity from a sector where people make employment choices based first and foremost on values. When you compete on the basis of how well your values connect with people it really sharpens your awareness of the value of the brand."

F – "There's a lot of focus on culture and fit when you first join. But then most of the rest is fluid, it happens all around you and isn't the sort of place where you switch into 'and now we'll talk about management time and develop a vision.' It's hard to describe but the brand and the vision are so dynamic they're happening while we speak."

G – "We're all very clear about where we've come from, the values that differentiate us and where we're going. We talk about the brand all the time and are pretty critical of marketing initiatives as we have a very firm view of what we are and what we aren't as a business."

C – "It's almost naff here to refer to terms that we associate with stuffiness or management speak or what our competitors do. We like to be different and unconstrained. But we certainly know what our brand's all about even if we don't always know what's next for the business. That's part of the edge of working here – we expect the unexpected and decisions which swim against the tide."

6. *It's at least as important to develop an **appropriate internal culture**, reflecting the brand, as it is to attract customers to it. Is culture something that is taken seriously here?*

F – "Oh yes. But culture's a loaded term. We're very much a melting pot as a business but there's a real sense that people matter big time. This is reflected in the facilities and how we're encouraged to work. It's less a place full of roles and more a place where peer pressure is obvious (and not the bullying kind)."

C – "It's what we're all about. It's really our brand USP. We know we work differently here than our competitors do. We out 'cool' the new entrants to the market, out 'smart' the more established players, and out 'perform' the cheaper players. There's little doubting that this is a people business as the perks are unique but it's not soft or overly indulgent either."

E – "Some criticize us for having an overly engineered culture. But at least you know where you stand and, as a member of staff, just like a customer, you choose to stay or leave with your eyes very much wide open. This isn't as innovative as some businesses but it's very rewarding to people who work hard. Can many other brands truly claim that this is the case?"

A – "It's everything to us. We monitor culture formally and informally throughout the business and ensure that we only recruit the right people."

B – "If you employ fans of your brand people already know what good behavior looks like and if they care about the brand they will do all they can for the cause. It becomes tribal – in a good way."

D – "We take our internal culture very seriously. We measure and monitor it alongside a suite of hard and soft performance indicators.

All line managers are responsible for keeping our culture in line with our brand promise and we try to do this one employee at a time rather than through mass marketing. This isn't just a nice-to-have part of our responsibilities as it is at other places I've worked."

G – "Absolutely. Our partnership ethos is everywhere from above the door through to all communication and the way we're paid and rewarded. It's fundamental to our brand. You know that when you join, it's made very very clear. There are plenty of alternatives if you want something different. Peer pressure (the good kind) helps to keep standards high."

7. *Brands are approximately **80% behavioral and 20% physical.** Brand management budgets should reflect this. What type of engagement activity do you get involved with?*

E – "I'm not sure that it feels like that split here. The physical brand, the logo and livery is really dominant, as are the processes and the way we work. I guess they mean nothing unless we, the employees, can support them. But this isn't an 80/20 business however you look at it really. Sure people make a huge difference at all levels but the infrastructure is so strong the brand is like a dominant force in its own right. Managers spend a lot of time sharing best practices and updating themselves via fresh training and this is cascaded to us on a regular basis."

C – "I'm not denying the physical brand is very sexy, potent, something to proudly be associated with. I love being at our parties, telling people where I work or even wearing our merchandise. But that's only because I'm confident that anyone sitting next to me on a plane or button holing me on holiday etc. probably has great stories to tell about the brand. That's down to the people who work there more than our products. So I would have to say I agree with the 80/20 rule. Much engagement activity is team based but it's fairly typical to see the top team turn up unannounced at celebrations and meetings. They like to 'catch people' doing things well, not catch them out. Our rewards for top performers are legendary, including holidays and travel. There's also a passionate back to the floor process for anyone in a 'management' position."

G – "That sounds about the right mix to me. No point in having great products and well-appointed stores if the staff are a nightmare. No point attracting people with adverts that promise one thing and then ruining it for the customers because of a poor delivery or shopping experience. I'm most interested in the things I can influence and leave the other stuff to the people who know best. I can be responsible for my own behavior and that of my team."

F – "Having a dominant brand can be a double-edged sword. People only really see the brand and tend to take the people who power the brand for granted, especially when there doesn't tend to be a direct customer relationship in most cases. But that's where staff/staff relations are vital I guess. If we can't change the physical nature of the brand we can certainly influence functionality. We can shape experiences. Our internal communications reflect this and utilize all electronic and traditional channels. There's a lot of focus on gatherings and socializing here, giving people a sense of belonging to a family that rates and invests in them."

A – "There's very little time spent internally considering the physical brand. It's very much secondary to how we show up at work. Our focus is on placing people on the frontline if we need to engage them, experiencing the effects of what we do rather than simulating it somewhere in a hotel or training facility."

B – "The two work in harmony but there's no brand without performance (at least not a brand we would want to be associated with). It's what gives us bragging rights."

D – "We have deliberately tried to downplay the over-promising aspect of many brands in our sector. We genuinely must spend more on employee engagement activities from our professional internal communications, induction, and training through to the events we have from time to time."

8. *Brand **engagement** takes place predominantly at an **emotional level** rather than a rational one, and internal communication needs to respect and reflect this not attempt to align employees. If you have an internal communication function, what's their brand engagement role?*

D – "We celebrate brand champions and ambassadors internally by highlighting and rewarding high-performing people. In an environment where measurement is key it's just part of the culture and is what people expect. Team briefings run by line managers are an important part of our internal communication process and feedback is channeled both ways at these. The twice yearly CEO updates are the big ticket pieces of communication but the day to day stuff is where most of it happens. We have all the usual channels from intranet through to area-specific newsletters but face-to-face communication is where most of the activity takes place, especially regarding big issues."

G – "We hold communication half hours which involve partners and feature high performers. There's a free press section on the intranet to encourage people to air their views and two partner newspapers to highlight good practice. Communication committees meet at every branch, not cascaded from the center."

B – "Communication is largely handled by one unit. We have access to the full range of media here but because we tend to be passionate about the brand we tend to seek out what we need to know rather than rely on spoon-feeding from a department."

A – "We take colleague communication very seriously. We don't pay what some organizations do but still attract the best people in many posts and their decisions to join tend to be values based. Internal communication used to be less professional than it is now but we have great online facilities, briefings and expect line supervisors to take the lead."

C – "As we keep our teams and units relatively small and informal there's an open environment here. We have a professional internal communications department and they provide us with the key messages but it's down to each of us to bring this to life. Any organization wide events do tend to be 'knock 'em dead' and are the envy of my friends."

E – "Like most things, this is very professionally managed and we have first-rate senior managers responsible for internal communication at the center. Locally, team briefings, simple bite-size sessions, are where most messages are received and feedback passed back."

D – "Our internal communication is seen as a benchmark for many organizations in our sector. It covers all channels from paper through to electronic and face-to-face with the emphasis on being factual and keeping it simple. First line supervisors lead the way, they're the hub."

F – "The most impressive thing here is the way people network with each other and the pace of moving something from feedback through to action. It doesn't happen via internal communications, whose role as far as I can tell is to coordinate the big ticket stuff. Key to communication for me is culture. You need to want to do it and then will use what vehicles there are to their best effect."

9. ***Authenticity*** *is the cornerstone of brand survival, and employees are far more sensitive to and intolerant of insincerity than customers. What does the organization do to enable you to be yourself?*

F – "This isn't an environment for bullshitters and frauds. The average employee is pretty intelligent, self-starting, initiative-taking, and technically proficient. If you can't fulfill these criteria this isn't the place for you. The company invests a hell of a lot in caring for the people who work here from Wi-Fi on the transport links to a fantastic and free canteen. It would be a bit disingenuous to not go the extra mile when they've tried so hard."

D – "This industry has been heavily criticized for promising one thing and practicing something else. We care a lot about sincerity in our dealings with customers and each other. We don't hook customers on price and then undermine our service promise with offshore call centers or relying on customer inertia. In our training and induction and in the feedback we receive, we are encouraged to be ourselves and to relate and empathize with customers. Only the best performing staff are promoted to supervise others. They have to lead by example and they pass these standards onto their mentees."

G – "We operate a no-individual-perks policy which encourages a team approach, and the strongly subsidized social and leisure facilities, which buck the trend away from what are seen as nonessential costs in many sectors, are very well received, as are the parties for partners and their families. When we do have to downsize, which is inevitable in today's business environment, we operate an above-state-minimum policy. It's easy to underestimate the positive effect this has on the rest of the staff. With the extent of benefits like these, it's easy to be yourself and personality is certainly encouraged in the way we role model the values to each other and customers, with the best sales people having well thought through facts, figures, and anecdotes about their products. Would the assistant in Tesco know that the vacuum cleaner you were considering was used in the White House?"

C – "Being real and approachable, being yourself, and giving enthusiasm and energy is expected here. After all it's role modeled right at the pinnacle of the business. People are encouraged to think out-side the box; to talk about what they do at home and the week-ends; to bring families to our celebrations; to empathize with customers when we're brainstorming and looking to shake things up. There's an absolute open-door policy here and no room for insincerity. This is enshrined in our Charter, which covers the group and links into group standards. It's very clear. And there's a customer service group to share learnings and best practice staffed by people like me."

A – "People have a voice at all levels of the organization and the flat structure discourages writing for the file and boss watching. There's nothing to be gained from making false promises inter-nally or externally and plenty to lose when decisions can liter-ally cost lives. And if our stakeholders ever got wind of anything approaching money wasting, it wouldn't just affect us but the whole sector. That sort of responsibility keeps you focused. There's a tremendous lack of cynicism here."

E – "There's a fine line between simply going through the motions and being genuine with customers. Colleagues are even harsher critics. We invest a lot in training aimed at helping our people become effective at customer service; communication; and yes, selling or providing value adding services. Much of this is car-ried out locally. Our staff know that their managers have all come through the system and they respect that."

10. *Brands are arguably filling in for traditional **sense-making** institutions like the state and religion as sources of identity and higher-order needs. How important is the workplace and the brand to helping make sense of life and creating a sense of purpose?*

E – "The impact of our brand is the stuff of legend. We arguably have a greater influence than many national leaders. The arrival of our brand is even heralded as the 'coming of civilization' in certain areas, whether we agree or not. We have a university and global events which feature some of the best musicians and enter-tainers. Our managers are incredibly loyal and passionately defend the brand and our approach. I guess it's relatively easy to suggest that our brand and our approach has its disciples both inside and out. We give a great deal back to charities and communities as well but are often the target of cynics and detractors, largely owing to the influence of the brand and its link to a particular ideology which not everyone shares."

B – "Our brand undoubtedly means a great deal to our loyal customer and staff base worldwide. It's respected and envied by our competitors. It's evolving all the time as the international market grows and we have a responsibility to 'share the love' by sending touring parties to places we ordinarily wouldn't have gone before. I'm not sure we create meaning but when people want to host their wedding at your premises, call their kids after your people, and name moments they've shared with you over and above key moments in their lives I guess you have to feel a sense of privilege and responsibility (if not challenging where their priorities should be)."

F – "The organization is not quite as big as many companies out there. But it has a huge user base. Most of what you work on will probably touch millions of people.

That's a pretty awesome and powerful thrill. I think of a small idea and collaborate with the team, they make it a reality and in a few days something that was just in your brain is now available to hundreds of thousands of people!

If I've helped create something that takes just a little bit of stress out of people's lives it's a powerful thing. This is light years ahead of how other companies drive change.

Our products are mostly free so you don't have to worry about the vagaries of trying to do things that are fluff or driven by other interests. You can focus on the customers.

Our brand is incredibly powerful in a sort of understated way. We're part of an information revolution. We do have a huge number of devotees but we don't encourage them in an extroverted or arrogant way. We just get a great buzz from helping them literally make sense of things in ever more convenient ways."

A – "We're all about helping people. Everything in the business has to be directed at helping people. We worry about whether we're making a difference constantly. We question our approaches and procedures endlessly. It's difficult to understate the impact it can have on a team to do something practical for people in trouble and if our people can do something to restore people's faith and trust and regain a sense of control, we've fulfilled our brand promise. Our role as brand champions is to spread that sense of value and worth throughout the business given only a limited number of us can be where the action is. Internal communication is vitally important to celebrate people, processes, and achievements internally using new media and face-to-face approaches."

C – "I'm not sure we help people make sense of life but through our core brand and brand extensions we like to think we bring a little extra spice and excitement into people's lives. And that starts with our own people. We have a brand quality director but it's really down to us all."

D – "Our industry brands and their employees used to be respected as one of the pillars of the community. That has been undermined in the main. But we have been trailblazers in this sector for many years and are still visited by organizations trying to learn about the way we connect with our employees and customers, how we manage relationships. When your brand is synonymous with efficiency and relationship management, you must be doing something right."

G – "Our brand is consistently used as a marker for how society is developing based upon people's shopping habits and how we appeal to a changing demographic. I wouldn't suggest that we're 'sense making' but we do offer a certain lifestyle to employees and customers. We wouldn't still be in business and performing counter to the recession if we weren't delivering, I guess."

Hopefully, through the simple device of removing the distraction of the logo and livery associated with their brand, the reader can focus on the valuable insights these seven brand champions are able to offer, confident in the knowledge that they represent the insights of brand leaders within leading brands.

These Magnificent Seven stories reassure me at least that it is eminently possible to influence the vast majority of employees to become equally passionate and practical brand champions by employing the relatively easy to follow brand engagement insights offered here. It's up to you how famous you allow yourself to become in the process or whether, like these seven champions, you feel it may be more effective or appropriate to elevate others while remaining behind the superhero cloak of anonymity yourself.

PART 5

REINFORCING A BRAND CHAMPION CULTURE

ARE BRAND CHAMPIONS MADE OR ARE THEY BORN?

As we've explored, brand is synonymous with reputation. If you accept my simple definition of a brand as stakeholder perception of promise minus delivery, then you have to accept that brands can be influenced or even managed. Third-party perceptions of brand performance and reputation are their reality whether they are true or not, but perceptions can certainly be molded over time. For a brand to be truly sustainable, the process of influencing perceptions has to start at home, with the employees and not with the advertising.

If brands are crafted, molded, nurtured, can brand champions be *created* or:

- is the desire to overdeliver *innate*?
- is it something employees either have or don't?
- are organizational superheroes *found* or are they *made*?
- are they the responsibility of *recruitment* or *management*?

Happily the answer is yes to all of the above, as we've shown throughout the case studies. To further illustrate this point, all three of the brand champions showcased next are driven by a strong sense of pride, have a powerful sense of their values, have a clean line of sight between those values and the brand and exude the RIPE characteristics all engaged brand champions share:

- **Receptive** (they are open to opportunities to be involved)
- **Involved** (they are part of the program not recipients of it)
- **Proactive** (they innovate without being asked)
- **Energized** (they do more things)

Outcomes
- **Achievement** (the things they do tend to be fruitful)
- **Advocacy** (they are proud and happy and actively recommend the brand to all four stakeholder communities)

While I believe that the will to achieve is innate, you shouldn't underestimate the influence organizations have on an employee's desire to do the right thing for customers. All the organizations featured next appreciate that a focus on employee engagement and recognition for outstanding performance can create a high performance culture. They also know that consistent high-performance is key to sustaining customer perceptions of their brand because they bother to measure the relationship between the two. They care about what customers and employees think, feel and subsequently do.

USING CUSTOMER FEEDBACK TO IDENTIFY AND MOTIVATE BRAND CHAMPIONS

As I've outlined, brand champions are everywhere but often taken for granted as they are usually right under our noses. Key questions, as I've mentioned, are:

- how do you find them?
- how do you define them?
- and how can you encourage more of the same?

One of the answers lies in bothering to seek and sustain customer feedback. Of course, data capture and mining can easily become an end in itself if you're not careful. It seldom requires a heavyweight or an overly sophisticated approach. But at its pragmatic best, by capturing, analyzing and acting on individual customer recognition stories, you should be able to:

- locate the practicing champions in all areas of your company
- influence internal brand advocacy levels
- clearly define what brand champions do that makes your customers value them so much
- inspire other employees to emulate the behaviors of the very best

- create a brand engaged culture in which employees strive to be recognized and rewarded for outstanding service

The Deming devotees will be thrilled to hear that it requires systemic thinking, blending quantitative analysis with qualitative insights. But measurement shouldn't be all that difficult if you're asking the right questions, role modeling your desired culture during the process, and looking in the right places.

I've been a fan of Sean McDade and Kate Feather of the US-based measurement company PeopleMetrics for some time. They have helped me prove the link between brand performance and employee engagement and between brand advocacy and business performance in a range of situations and circumstances.

PeopleMetrics is a leading research and technology firm helping companies engage customers, employees and, interestingly, physicians to drive bottom line results. Long before it was fashionable to do so, we shared a core passion for embracing the touchy feely people disciplines but lending them backbone and substance by encouraging consistent, enlightening and repeatable measurement.

Through a combination of the RIPE AA criteria detailed earlier as key indicators of engaged employees and the PeopleMetrics nGauge, which measures:

- purpose
- trust
- growth
- fun
- recognition
- resources
- rewards

to uncover engagement levers, we're able to identify where to prioritize the engagement effort. This type of analysis, along with customer feedback, supports the successes of internal brand champions by providing continuous signals from stakeholder communities and guidance on the *best actions* to take in response to specific comments and challenges. The stories of the brand champions that follow were largely informed by stakeholder feedback obtained by striving to identify key stakeholder engagement levers.

Heroes in the headlines

On January 15, 2009, US Airways Flight 1549 hit a flock of Canada geese and was forced to crash-land in the Hudson River. New York Governor David Paterson quickly branded the incident "The Miracle on the Hudson" and the extraordinary survival of all 155 people on board made international headlines. This potential tragedy was averted by the heroically named Chesley B. (Sully) Sullenberger III, dubbed "one of Gotham's brightest heroes, able to land engineless airplanes in a single try" (*The New York Daily News*, January 16, 2009).

The headlines about the incident made it easy for US Airways Chief Executive Doug Parker to find and recognize some of his very best, and obvious, brand champions, Sully and his crew. But no employer would wish to rely on such exceptional (and dangerous) circumstances to identify and celebrate their best talent. After all, thousands of pilots and crew land millions of passengers safely daily without dramatic incident. Few, thankfully, are faced with such overtly heroic circumstances, but brand champions abound nevertheless.

The anecdotal heroes

All too often it is the grandstanders, the C suite, political favorites or the lucky employees in the right place at the right time who get recognized by leadership and receive the better career opportunities.

These "anecdotal heroes" typically work in organizations where high performers are identified internally by managers and leaders, rather than externally by customers.

This method is rife with problems. One of them is the potential *dis*engagement, resentment and cynicism it can create among the less visible, yet often equally talented individuals who feel overlooked.

As Kate Feather points out:

Over the years, across hundreds of thousands of employee engagement surveys, we have heard employees speak of the "old boys club," office "politics," "unclear selection criteria" and "favoritism" as causes of disengagement.

Many feel that persons are promoted because they fit in with the "old boys club"... some of the promotions over the last few months have been bad enough to make others want to leave, yet there does not seem to be any standard on what it takes to get ahead – except poor performance and being cool with the right manager.

It is very frustrating that you can do an outstanding job, but because you don't deal with the field offices, etc. you very rarely get acknowledged.

Too many times I have seen exceptional employees passed up for promotion due to "politics."

A great morale booster would be to increase recognition of individual efforts and achievements regardless of location. Unfortunately, many of us feel that unless we are in a high-profile location..., opportunities for recognition just are not there as they are for other business units.

Rather than relying exclusively on feedback from internal managers and leaders, your customers can be the best source for naming your brand champions.

Customer branded champions

When customer feedback is used to identify and share brand champion stories, the usual method is to post customer letters praising members of staff on bulletin boards, in newsletters and on the intranet.

This approach, however, requires customers to take the initiative to tell the organization about their experience and share their appreciation, and diligent recipients to do something with the feedback. In other words, you have to wait for the customer to brand your champions for you and rely on ad hoc actions to spread the word.

The PeopleMetrics research backs up the unfortunate truism that a person will exert themselves to tell you about a poor experience much more often than a good one. Therefore, if you rely on your customers to be sufficiently motivated to share their positive experiences with you, or worse yet you depend entirely on managers to identify the heroes in their midst, many great stories will be missed and many brand heroes will go unnoticed. Covert operations are fine, but they're difficult to sustain and you can't replicate what you don't know about.

SYSTEMATICALLY UNMASKING YOUR HEROES

Every day in your organization, employees are positively affecting customers in grand and modest ways. The challenge you face from a brand development perspective is being able to *systematically* uncover these situations and methodologies behind them to make your business stronger.

One of the best ways to unearth your brand champions is to systematically solicit feedback from your customers. Asking the people who experience your service and your brand about their experience allows you to:

- *recognize and reward all the heroes* – not just those you hear about by chance or are already familiar with. This can create a more engaged employee base that sees a fair and just reward and recognition structure.
- mine this feedback to *identify the employee behaviors* that your customers appreciate the most and use it to inform training programs, hiring practices and performance management discussions.
- *encourage more of these desired behaviors* as positive customer feedback and recognition becomes something to strive for.
- *quantify the link* between engagement, "heroic" behaviors and the customer experience, thereby lending greater weight to the argument for *investing in people.*

Through customer engagement work with three brands in particular – Christie's Auction House, Signature Flight Support and Wise Consulting Associates – we can see firsthand evidence of how proactively soliciting customer feedback can reveal the employees who are best representing their brand every day.

CHRISTIE'S FINDS A MASTERPIECE

Christie's, the world's leading art business, had global auction and private sales in 2008 that achieved £2.8bn/$5.1bn. Christie's is a brand and place that speaks of extraordinary art, unparalleled service and expertise, as well as international glamour. Christie's may not feature as a Global Top 10 Brand but few would argue about its brand credentials.

Founded in 1766 by James Christie, Christie's conducted the greatest auctions of the eighteenth, nineteenth and twentieth centuries, and today remains a popular showcase for the unique and the beautiful. Christie's offers hundreds of sales annually in over 80 categories, including all areas of fine and decorative arts, jewelry, photographs, collectibles, wine and more. Prices range from $200 to over $80mn.

Christie's has 57 offices in 32 countries and 10 salerooms around the world, including in London, New York, Paris, Geneva, Milan, Amsterdam, Dubai and Hong Kong. Christie's leads the market with initiatives in growing geographic regions as well as categories and value ranges of sales.

You don't sustain a brand like Christie's for 250 years without exceptional people and an array of brand advocates. In recent years Christie's has been able to recognize its brand champions through systematically inviting feedback from its clients. Christie's may be a premier brand name but its refined image, rather like that of the graceful swan on the pond, belies a great deal of ongoing hard work beneath the surface.

Vision: Christie's is a name and place that speaks of extraordinary art, unparalleled service and expertise, as well as international glamour.

Mission: Christie's is the world's leading art business in terms of sales, profitability and quality of works of art offered.

Values: Christie's core values are:

- passionate expertise
- exceptional customer service
- business judgment
- integrity
- teamwork
- innovation

These core values embody the key behaviors that are required from employees.

Christie's approach to creating and sustaining brand champions is, like the best ideas, relatively simple. Clients receive a short online or paper survey following a recent registration, purchase or consignment at one of the 500+ sales hosted by Christie's in any given year. Within the survey, clients are invited to name and describe a Christie's employee who went above and beyond for them.

As client feedback has been collected over the years, one brand champion has repeatedly surfaced at their flagship US operation. It's not one of the high-profile auctioneers or account managers, as one might expect.

Gil Perez is the doorman at Christie's Rockefeller Plaza headquarters in New York City. He has been at Christie's for close to thirty years and is recognized by clients as an "ambassador," an "icon," a "people person extraordinaire!" and some claim he is the "greatest doorman in the history of New York City." Gil is a brand superhero beyond compare.

Interestingly, Gil wasn't always the visible ambassador of Christie's. Oddly enough he started out in Security of all places. Within a few short years in this role, however, he managed to foster immense internal trust. He also managed to learn the business from the inside out. He had the keys and combinations to all of the locks. He was asked to pick up precious works of art from the airport. He opened and locked up the building on a regular basis. He literally safeguarded the family silver on countless occasions. The trust and empowerment that were handed down to Gil clearly helped cultivate a strong bond between the man and the brand.

Management's confidence in and reliance on Gil in this position meant that he met with resistance to securing a front-of-house position (the age old paradox of overloading the willing horse). But, Gil

---

What clients have to say about Gil

"I was also impressed by the kind doorman who hailed a taxi and helped me into it with the sculpture, and he wouldn't even accept a tip."

"... especially the doorman named Gil, who I have known for over 25 years. [He] is a very special person who makes everyone feel great and he knows everybody's name."

"The greatest doorman in New York's history greets everyone in a way that makes us feel happy and valued."

"Gil the doorman [...] is the friendly face – and – in fact an icon for Christies in NY."

"Gil Perez is a fantastic ambassador for Christies."

says, he got a lucky break. He was fortunate enough to be on first name terms with most of the senior leaders. After making his case with François Curiel, the then President of the New York auction house, he was given a six-month trial on the door. In the end, that was the best decision Curiel could have made, as he transferred Gil's back-office qualities, which had been hidden under the proverbial bushel, to front of house. Gil became the first public face of Christie's that most customers saw.

Gil embraced the opportunity he had been given. Most importantly, Gil utilized his skills as an observer and a learner. During the early weeks in his new job, after willingly putting in 15-hour days, Gil would walk to the best hotels in the city and watch the doormen there. He'd stand opposite the Waldorf, the Regency and the Park Plaza. He scrutinized and analyzed what he saw. He picked up best practices where he could but, surprisingly, Gil didn't discover what to do as a great doorman; he learned what *not* to do. He saw doormen talking to each other, standing away from the curb, leaning against the wall, smoking, only greeting the clients as they disembarked from their cars. Gil decided there was a better way.

Gil's way is to stand out in front, greet all clients by name and with a warm smile. He remembers a fact or tidbit about them, sends personal greeting cards, parks cars, hails cabs, charms the New York City traffic cops on the customer's behalf, hand delivers important works to incapacitated clients in need of a home viewing, and carries valuable pieces across city blocks in all types of weather.

And how does he manage all of this? He doesn't have any particularly advanced skills or training. He has no customer service superpowers. What Gil does, most people could do if they cared enough about the time they invest at work or stopped hanging up their personalities when they signed in at work.

Gil's observation skills extend to Christie's client base. Since the beginning, without prompting, he has jotted down facts about regular clients, noting who always wears his lucky tie or who has a particular gait. As this information grew, Gil created his own client database. Gil is a people person, not a computer guy, and this was no SQL database. Gil's database, which he continues to build today, lives on the walls of his 12 × 12 locker room, where he places his own notes written on the business cards of more than 2000 clients, organized by art specialty.

Christie's recognizes that Gil is special – so special that a number of years ago they promoted him to Assistant Vice President. They believe he embodies their values (as noted above):

- passionate expertise
- exceptional customer service
- business judgment
- integrity
- teamwork
- innovation

Importantly, they want to ensure that Gil spreads his behavioral DNA as far as possible throughout the group to create a culture of "living the Christie's brand" and they have flown him to train other doormen, even in London.

Because Gil knows practically everyone and is able to connect with clients on a personal level, he was recently asked to serve as an ambassador of Christie's at one of their most important sales in Venice. In many respects, Gil is the walking and talking embodiment of the Christie's brand, an advocate with highly contagious qualities.

The positive feedback received from Christie's clients has helped to reinforce Gil's importance to the organization. At the time of writing this, Gil has been intending to retire from the door so he can spend more time with his grandson. But somehow, he, and Christie's, just can't let go.

SIGNATURE NAMES TOP GUNS AND LOYALTY SOARS

Signature Flight Support is the largest supplier of aviation services to individuals and business customers internationally. Signature has made a point of identifying individual brand champions, encouraging more employees to deliver superior service, and, in so doing, increasing customer loyalty.

Vision: Signature Flight Support's vision is to be a dynamic, world-class supplier to the global aerospace industry, continuously delivering exceptional performance.

Mission: The company's mission is to grow exceptional, long-term, sustainable value for their stakeholders through:

- exceeding customer expectations and competitor offerings
- continuously improving market-leading and innovative businesses
- working together for greater gain
- being an employer of choice for empowered individuals in a safe and sustainable environment
- always behaving with integrity and respect

To support its vision and mission, Signature's core values are:

Integrity	We earn the trust and respect of our stakeholders with honesty, fairness, openness and by achievement of our commitments
Responsibility	Managing our impact on, and contributing positively to, society and the environment
Safety	We are dedicated to safety and security, the elimination of hazards and protecting people, property and our environment
Service	We strive continually to anticipate customer needs, exceeding their expectations
People	We embrace diversity and equality, investing in and empowering our people through training, education, and experience
Performance	We focus on delivery of long-term and sustainable value, continuous improvement, and reliability

With 80+ locations worldwide, and a focus on competing for service, Signature has been collecting customer feedback and measuring customer loyalty since 2006. They believe that a systemic approach to data collection is invaluable to provide focus for their brand champions. For Signature, a loyal customer is one who willingly acts as a brand advocate, recommends Signature to others and intends to visit them again in the future.

Part of the Signature Customer Engagement Management approach includes collecting and sharing customer recognition stories through real-time Recognition Alerts. When a customer shares how a Signature employee went above and beyond for them, a real-time Recognition Alert is sent to various leaders' and managers' inboxes, largely to ensure that best practices are disseminated as quickly as possible as well as to recognize individual achievements. These employees are thanked by their location manager and, if they receive multiple such alerts, are publicly rewarded and recognized at the end of the year. Through this effort, Signature has been able to track customer loyalty and advocacy at the location level and uncover and reinforce the behavior of brand champions. Within the open and extrovert culture of the airline business this recognition technique receives a great deal of positive feedback from Signature employees.

One of these employees is Sandy Tachovsky, a customer service representative (CSR) at Signature's Minneapolis/St. Paul location.

Sandy joined Signature as a CSR in 1989 after working as a substitute teacher. Similar to Gil at Christie's, Sandy approached this new role with study and observation before jumping in feet first.

When she started, she made her own cut-and-paste aviation book so she could understand the different aircraft and connect with the pilots as they came into the facility. Sandy also took the initiative to make a special connection with her customers. She started, and continues, to send handwritten notes to customers she hasn't seen for a while or

---

What customers have to say about Sandy

"I arrived at 7:30am and needed transportation to downtown ... for a business meeting. No line crew members were available, so Sandy just grabbed her coat and jumped in the car, giving me a quick ride and allowing me to arrive on time for a significant 8:00am meeting and presentation with the Board of Trustees."

"Sandy went above and beyond what is expected and made us look like superstars to our passengers with transportation, catering, etc. She really understands customer service and was very good at communicating and understanding our needs."

"Those members of your staff [Sandy, Emily, Annette, Bob, Ryan and Kristy] know me and have gone out of their way to be ahead of me on every visit."

to acknowledge a recent visit. Sandy's customers recognize her for her professionalism, empathy, ability to anticipate their needs and commitment to going the extra mile on their behalf. They're clearly touched by the very human and personable way she bothers to get to know them, a contrast to an age of cold calling, call centers and machines.

Sandy's secret is her attitude, something that can never be conscripted or trained. She takes pride in what she does. Her colleagues say they've never seen her in a bad mood. The frequent positive feedback from customers, reinforced using Signature's systematic techniques, has led Signature to recognize Sandy in a variety of ways.

She was recently invited to Washington, DC, to be involved in the 2009 Presidential Inauguration activities at Signature and has been invited to attend other customer focused events to interact with some of Signature's most important clients. And Sandy's renown goes further than Signature and their customers. Every year since 2004, Sandy has been named one of the top ten customer service representatives in the nation by *Pro-Pilot* magazine.

Sandy says that she strives to give 100% each day and is gratified when she gets positive feedback from customers at the location or through Signature's customer feedback efforts. Sandy says feedback is motivating because *"I like knowing that what I have done has helped the customer. You always want to do a good job. You always want to strive to be better. And then when you get the feedback it's even more motivating. Customer recognition makes good service contagious ... and you can see the other CSRs striving to be recognized in that way too."*

How does Signature know that focusing on customer recognition is helping them improve? The data say so:

■ this motivation to do well and to receive positive accolades from customers is spreading across Signature Flight Support's locations. Since introducing the Recognize Alert system, the proportion of Signature clients that are considered advocates of the Signature brand, essentially as loyal as you can get, has increased by six percentage points and exceeds best-in-class levels.

■ analysis of the correlation between customer recognition and customer loyalty has revealed that the locations with the highest proportion of Recognition Alerts also have the highest levels of customer loyalty. Figure 31 depicts this relationship. All of Signature's locations have been grouped according to the volume of Recognition Alerts received from their customers. The locations that fall into the top

10% with regard to recognition have significantly higher customer loyalty (72%). This drops by 14 points when one looks at the lowest performing locations with regard to customer recognition.

How else is Signature learning from this feedback? Signature's Vice President of Customer Relations puts it this way:

Over the course of time, through the survey process, we've learned where we should allocate our assets and finance. The analysis reveals our key drivers – where we should focus – and what we should emphasize in training. For us, and our customers, we've learned that it's all about the soft skills.

One other great advantage in taking a methodical approach to identifying an organization's brand champions is the ability to measure that which leaders say they know but don't necessarily always support – the value of the "most important asset," the company employee. The Signature experience proves the value of supporting soft skills with hard data and how brand champions have a disproportionately positive impact on the local culture and in turn brand perceptions.

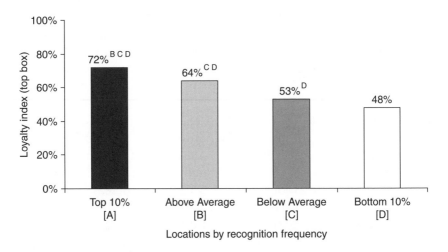

FIGURE 31 **Signature's employee recognition and customer loyalty results**

Note: Letters denote statistically significant differences between groups. That is, the top 10% of locations (denoted with an A) based on proportion of Recognition Alerts received have a significantly higher customer loyalty index than all other locations (denoted with B, C and D).

WISE CONSULTING'S SAGE APPROACH

Wise Consulting Associates, a Baltimore, Maryland, based HR and payroll consulting firm, was able to correlate employee centered actions and programs (an expense) with clients' perceptions of the value Wise delivers (and the associated long-term revenue stream). They did this through a deliberate approach to measuring both client and associate engagement. Leadership's belief was that the more engaged a consultant, the greater the level of advocacy and the better the ultimate experience for the client. In order to reinforce this belief they deliberately tracked the correlation between employee engagement and customer perceptions of service and in turn the brand.

The results demonstrated that corporate actions around, and investment in, associate engagement can drive higher levels of individual effort and ultimately create legions of willing brand advocates internally and externally.

The Employee Engagement index used by Wise Consulting is calculated using four questions to measure:

- retention
- extra effort
- advocacy
- passion

Associates are engaged if they agree or strongly agree with all four questions. As Figure 32 depicts, a ten-point gap differentiates the level of engagement among those receiving the most client recognition (the brand champions) from that of the rest of the associates.

While both associate and client engagement is exceptionally high at Wise, the more engaged associates received the highest volume of Recognition Alerts from clients – clearly demonstrating their effectiveness as brand champions and the link between engagement, advocacy and performance.

One hundred percent of those individuals "strongly agreed" they are willing to "give extra effort" (vs. 87% of the others). Wise leadership believes this is the most significant factor in motivating clients to subsequently recognize these individuals.

Just as the existence of self-managing teams signals a highly engaged culture, volunteering extra effort and taking individual initiative to go the extra mile is the cornerstone of the fully engaged brand champion. Wise brand champions prove the rule.

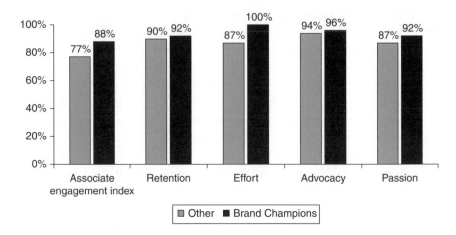

FIGURE 32   **The Wise brand champions data**

Charles Keyser, a long-term senior consultant at the organization, is continually recognized by his clients for his commitment and dedication to giving extra effort almost every time.

Through the associate engagement survey effort, Wise learned that to most improve levels of engagement of its staff, it needs to focus on

---

What clients have to say about Charles

"Charles Keyser always goes above and beyond. I have needed his assistance at the nth hour and he always helps me out even if it means 'squeezing' my project or issue in the middle of several other projects that he is working on."

"Charles held up his family from leaving on a scheduled vacation to make sure our year end W-2 information was correct and our needs were met."

"Many times, we have been in the middle of a process, gotten stuck and had to call on Charles to help us. Even when he has been out of the office, he checks messages regularly and consistently responds immediately to our urgent calls for help. One time in particular, it was late one evening and I was having trouble with an import that he had helped me with. I sent an urgent email to Charles, hoping he would be near his computer. Well, he was and he got back to me almost immediately. That is exceptional service and quality that I value highly. I know that we can count on Charles to provide exceptional quality and exceptional customer service."

---

providing a strong sense of purpose for the work being performed. To help associates be successful, people needed a context, a reason why the brand existed, a story and the goals and objectives the business was striving to achieve.

As Charles put it:

Because I approach work-related issues and situations with a combination of personal pride, a belief I can solve any problem, and an attitude of "it's just the right thing to do" for the client, Wise's culture and type of work are perfect for someone like me. In this environment, exceeding expectations becomes the norm.

Clearly Charles's values reinforce and complement those of the business.

The process of uncovering brand champions may differ between cultures. But with a judicious application of some simple measurement (signaling what is important) and some engaging, authentic, people based initiatives it can and should be done.

TOP CASE STUDY TIPS:

What Wise, Signature and Christie's have in common is a strong belief at leadership level that there is:

■ a close correlation between employee advocacy and customer satisfaction

■ a subsequent and incremental rise in customer advocacy

■ a compelling need to track the drivers of and relationship between both

■ a strong relationship between organization values and on-brand culture development

■ a strong link between sustainable brand development and constructive culture

■ a great deal to be gained from identifying and promoting internal brand champions

Referencing Campbell's archetypes once again, the brand development journey, whether traveled within marble halls or conducted largely in cyber space, will doubtless involve encounters with brand archetypes of one form or another. By creating the conditions in which employees are empowered and able to become actively involved and engaged enough to care, there's every likelihood that organizations will create enough brand advocates to transform customer perceptions and sustain brand reputation.

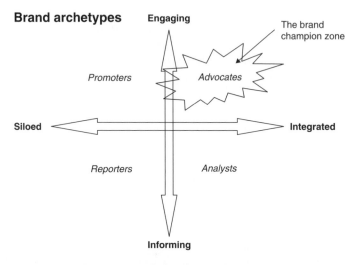

FIGURE 33   **The TBT brand archetype model**

Our next story, which reinforces the link between advocacy and brand development, comes from the other side of the Atlantic and tells the tale of the evolution of one of Britain's legendary fashion brands and how it is brought to life daily by brand champions at every level of the organization.

INSIDE BARBOUR

Barbour is one of Britain's iconic brands. Barbour began trading in 1894 and from the very early days quickly gained a reputation as a manufacturer and subsequently retailer of high-quality outerwear that would protect the wearer against the worst of the elements.

Barbour makes a lot of its legacy and its story began with John Barbour, who was born and raised on a farm in Galloway in west Scotland, the second son of a family whose history can be traced back to the fourteenth century. The ability of Barbour's leadership to reference their roots helps a great deal in the face of the trials and tribulations they have confronted together in a highly competitive industry. It helps convey a history of innovation, self-belief and tenacity – qualities which have helped the business adapt and thrive.

At the age of 20, John Barbour left the farm to try his luck across the border in the northeast of England, where in 1870 he started business as a traveling draper. A year later, he married his childhood sweetheart, Margaret Haining, who bore him 11 children and gave him the encouragement and belief to start J. Barbour & Sons in 1894 in 5 Market Place, South Shields.

The shop sold all manner of products loosely described as drapery, including outerwear, boiler suits and painter's jackets through to underwear, and, in the flourishing town of South Shields, the shop which became known as "Barbour's" thrived.

Almost from the first, Barbour derived an important part of its income from the ship owners, ship builders and seamen of the port, supplying Beacon brand oilskin coats designed to protect the growing community of sailors, fishermen, and river, dock and shipyard workers from the worst of the weather. They weren't the sort of customers to tolerate shoddy workmanship.

By 1906, Barbour was a successful business and John Barbour made two of his sons, Jack and Malcolm, equal partners in the business. The younger brother, Malcolm, expanded the business to supply Beacon oilskin clothing to landowners, farmers, farm workers and shepherds. He also produced the first Barbour catalog in 1908, which as well as targeting seamen and farmers focused on fishermen, forming the core of its future business.

By 1917, the mail order catalog accounted for almost 75% of Barbour's business, including international orders from as far away as Chile, South Africa and Hong Kong.

In 1912 J. Barbour & Sons became J. Barbour & Sons Ltd. with John Barbour as Chairman and Jack and Malcolm as joint Managing Directors. John remained as Chairman until he died on July 7, 1918, and was succeeded by Jack Barbour. In 1927 Jack resigned, leaving Malcolm to run the business. In 1919, Malcolm introduced the

Barbour's Buying Agency, which was founded to enable Barbour's to act as purchasing agents – buying and supplying any goods that Barbour was unable to provide directly from the shop or the catalog on behalf of anyone living overseas. This quite often proved to be a challenge, with requests as obscure as half a dozen penny mousetraps to be sent to Tibet, or half a ton of ship's biscuits to be sent to the Indian Ocean, but it reinforced the commitment that Barbour had to customer service which is still so important today.

In 1928 Duncan Barbour, Malcolm's only son, joined the business, having learned his trade at Bainbridge's, Newcastle's biggest department store.

During the First World War, demand was high in the army for oil-skins and Barbour continued to grow. However, following the war, with a general downturn in the economy and the Great Depression of 1929, the company's sales fell significantly and didn't recover until 1935, when the economy improved and Barbour started making a profit again.

Duncan Barbour, a keen motorcyclist himself, introduced a motor-cycling range in the 1930s which quickly took off. Barbour suits were worn by virtually every British international team from 1936 to 1977, when Barbour made the decision to pull out of the motorcycle clothing market. In 1957, 97% of all competitors who took part in the Scottish 6 Day Event rode in Barbour International Oiled Cotton suits.

With the start of the Second World War, Duncan was called away to fight and Malcolm Barbour took over full responsibility for Barbour again with the help of Duncan's wife, Nancy. Again, they produced weatherproof outdoor clothing for both the military and civilians, including the development of the Ursula suit, which became standard issue for members of the Submarine Service. The Ursula suit was named after the U-class submarine *Ursula*, whose commander, Captain George Philips, was instrumental in getting the suits produced.

Upon Duncan's return in November 1945, he set about expanding the business. The existing premises were becoming too small and antiquated to cope with the amount of business, and Duncan believed that the way forward was to build a manufacturing plant. In August 1957, Barbour moved to the Simonside Trading Estate on the outskirts of South Shields and after 63 years of being a retailer, Barbour became manufacturers and marketeers.

Duncan sadly never got to see the manufacturing plant; having overseen all the plans for the factory, he collapsed and died on June 15, age 48.

Malcolm again took over the reins with Nancy and her son, John, age 19. It was a difficult time for the company but sales continued to grow. In 1964, Malcolm Barbour died age 83 and Nancy Barbour took over the role of Chairman, with John as Joint Managing Director.

Then tragically in June 1968, while on holiday, John suffered a brain hemorrhage and died, leaving behind his young widow, Margaret, and their two-year-old daughter, Helen.

It was left to Margaret, a teacher by profession who up until this point had had no real involvement in Barbour, to pick up the reins and take control of the company's future. She was made a member of the Board of Directors, inheriting her husband's share of the company, and immersed herself in understanding all areas of the business, getting to know Barbour customers firsthand and talking to dealers about how they viewed the company and its way of doing business.

Margaret and her management team introduced new manufacturing and operational systems and throughout the 1970s efficiency and productivity increased and sales were buoyant. In 1972, Margaret Barbour was appointed company Chairman and in 1973 the company took the decision to discontinue all direct selling. The famous catalogs would continue but would now be used to support the product range, dealers and sales agents, with the focus on countrywear.

During the early 1990s, the business continued to expand internationally. Barbour won three Queen's Awards for Export Achievement in 1992, 1994 and 1995. From 2000, the company began to build a far wider comprehensive country clothing collection for men and women, moving into breathable waterproofs alongside the established wax jackets, and introduced a wider range of colors, including navy and sandstone, alongside the traditional olive and sage.

Margaret's daughter, Helen Barbour, was made Deputy Chairman in 1997, and in 1999 the first Barbour "shop in shop" opened in Harrods.

Today Barbour's headquarters are still in South Shields. Although it sources products from around the globe, Barbour's classic wax jackets are still manufactured by hand in the factory in Simonside and each year over 100,000 jackets are processed via the central, subsidiary and local customer service operations.

There are now over 2000 products across the two seasons and the collections now also cater for ladies and children.

Barbour now has 12 of its own retail shops in the UK, and a presence in 40 countries worldwide, including Germany, the Netherlands, Austria, France, the US, Italy, Spain, Argentina, New Zealand and Japan.

Broadening out from its countrywear roots, today the company produces clothing that is designed for a full country lifestyle. As well as jackets and coats, the Barbour wardrobe includes trousers, shirts, socks, midlayers and knitwear. Recently the brand was tipped as one to watch as younger customers discover Barbour's unique benefits.

Nevertheless, in whichever area the company now operates, it remains true to its history and core values as a family business with heroic forebears which espouses the unique values of the British countryside and brings the qualities of wit, grit and glamour to its beautifully functional clothing.

In the 1980s Barbour became a household name for its olive wax jackets and its association with the royal family and "Sloane rangers." It was an image that could easily have become a straitjacket for the Barbour business and brand, which has had to unfreeze certain ingrained brand perceptions without betraying its roots.

As the brand has introduced more product offerings, and the proposition to the consumer has evolved, it has become important to reposition the brand to reflect these changes. This is an ongoing challenge but is being achieved via segmentation of the product into four categories – heritage, contemporary, classic and sporting – and, most importantly, by reshaping the way the business engages with its employees to move with the times without losing touch with the culture that made Barbour what it is.

The heritage range includes garments that are based on Barbour's legacy; for example, the International jacket is based on an iconic motorcycle pattern from the 1930s. But today's heritage consumer is younger, more aware of classic design and more fashion savvy.

Contemporary garments are more on-trend (currently shorter and more fitted) and appeal to the 25+ consumer. Global fashion department stores have been particularly important in growing this range.

Classic garments reflect traditional styles and comfortable fits and are timeless.

The sporting range, as the name implies, covers sports such as shooting, walking and equestrianism, with functional elements in the clothing and technical features.

In using segmentation, Barbour's challenge is how to tailor brand communication to each segment. This is achieved through the use of advertising, advertorial and PR in different magazines for each segment. For example, Barbour's latest shooting jacket is advertised in *The Field* or *Shooting Gazette*, and their heritage range in fashion magazines such as *GQ* or *Elle*.

PR is also important in placing the right products in relevant magazines to attract the target market. As segmentation develops, distribution also becomes key in terms of the right product offering for the right retailer, and whereas in the past all products would have been offered to all retailers as the range was small, now it has had to become selective and more targeted.

From the beginning, the company focused on the principles of:

- quality
- durability
- fitness for purpose
- attention to detail

in everything that they produced. These principles still run through to the heart of everything Barbour does to this day.

Barbour has been on quite a journey and eventually evolved into a lifestyle brand. The classic wax jackets remain at the core of the business. They are Barbour's cornerstone products and physical legacy. But a new range of contemporary jackets in wax, waterproof breathable fabrics, quilts and wool, together with shirts, trousers, knitwear and accessories, have expanded the range and introduced Barbour to a new, younger target audience. The new products, however, just like the younger Barbour employees, still epitomize the founding principles, which are just as true today as they were back in 1894.

How are employees engaged with the Barbour brand?

Because of the virtually iconic status of the Barbour brand, most new recruits are very familiar with the core brand traits before they join. That's one of the advantages of a long and successful legacy.

On joining Barbour, without fail, all employees have a thorough induction, which importantly includes a history of the company. They became part of the strong narrative, building and conveying the Barbour brand legacy. Unlike many competitors Barbour doesn't just look forward but actively embraces what's great about their past. It gives the workforce tremendous confidence during the tough times, and, interestingly, when you talk to them many Barbour staff cite the case of the Kraft takeover of Cadbury's or the problems suffered by legacy financial services brands like Northern Rock and Royal Bank of Scotland as examples of what happens when a brand loses its way.

As a fourth generation family-owned company, it is important that employees understand the ethos and culture of the company, where from the Chairman downwards there is a passion for the product and the desire to do things right.

It is important that people understand where their role fits in and the importance of every individual's contribution to the company's success and how it merges into the departmental and bigger company picture. Simple, focused and authentic internal communication is key.

Perhaps unusually in these days when few CEOs seem to see further than 18 months ahead and the term performance culture suggests deliverables tied to reports to the demanding shareholders, there is a five-year plan that is communicated throughout the organization linked explicitly to the company vision for all employees.

The Managing Director, Steve Buck, believes in open and regular communication to update management on the short-, medium- and long-term objectives and insists that local leaders follow his example. They supplement this face-to-face communication with a company newsletter, notice boards and the intranet. Relatively simple but effective communication channels suffice and they take great pains to emphasize joined-up thinking and simplicity, stressing that retailing is essentially a simple case of selling products that people want and recommend or advocate.

The relationship between Marketing, HR, and the CEO's office and the role of this partnership in facilitating employee brand engagement

Within Barbour, unusually in these days of empire building, HR is not represented as a specific strategic function. There is, however, a manager employed to focus upon employee engagement and recruitment of employees with appropriate skills and experience, who will help to develop the brand in the appropriate direction. Employee engagement and responsibility for the development of people sits predominantly with the line managers with assistance from the aforementioned manager.

In 2005, however, Barbour recognized the need for the implementation of a new employee engagement strategy. The company was changing rapidly from a manufacturing only organization to market-facing brand actively looking to manage its profile in the fast changing consumer world.

To help manage the behavioral and physical aspects of the brand, Barbour introduced a relatively simple change management program with the following goals:

- to develop the skills of the leadership team to ensure it was capable of facilitating the growth of the brand in line with its strategy to allow all employees at varying levels to reach their best potential
- to create a sense of teamwork within and between departments
- to engender an awareness of the bigger picture and help people understand their role within that
- to drive higher morale, leading to even greater cooperation, motivation and engagement across the Barbour business

The change management program identified areas where changes to processes could be made that would improve functions and facilitate business efficiencies without introducing unsustainable outsourcing. Ultimately these fed into the broader business objectives of increasing sales and profitability and generally shaping the business for the future.

Rather than continue to rely on relaying Barbour principles and practices like cascading lore by word of mouth through generations, Barbour recognized that the business of managing the brand and driving through change would require greater degrees of ongoing consultation and a bit more systems thinking.

Three groups were set up involving employees (management and nonmanagement) to focus on the following key enabling areas:

- communication
- training and development
- leadership

The Communications group was established to look at improving connections between departments. One of the projects they undertook was called "Netiquette."

Netiquette at Barbour

It had become apparent that a worrying trend had developed and a growing amount of internal communication was being carried out by email. This was especially worrying within an organization which prides itself on employee communication and strong first-person communication with customers.

A campaign was launched via central and local presentations, posters on notice boards, the employee restaurant and other public places to raise awareness of the issue and to promote best practice. Netiquette encouraged employees to communicate face to face or by telephone rather than just relying on email, stressing the importance of role modeling the Barbour values. Netiquette was successful at getting employees to think about whether sending that email was necessary or simply discourteous and has encouraged employees to get up and talk to colleagues in a different department rather than just relying on the electronic message dumping chute.

Although fearsomely loyal at times, each of the three groups identified areas for improvement. While there were a range of quick wins identified in internal communication, the Training and Development team focused on performance management. The Leadership group developed and implemented a coherent set of company values – expanding on the core principles of working effectively and behaving appropriately to encourage consistency across all levels in the company.

As part of the change management process, Barbour introduced the 3C's FOR IT to act as the focal values for the brand awareness program, which every employee has been through and all new employees undertake. There are eight Barbour values in total:

- Consistency
- Clarity
- Commitment
- Fairness
- Openness
- Respect
- Integrity
- Trust

The brand and values workshops explore what these terms mean in practice from both the corporate and individual perspective and how they apply to stories of everyday life at Barbour. They are used to explore what a brand champion looks and feels like and to reinforce that a Barbour brand champion:

- is enthused and passionate
- wears the brand personally as well as professionally (advocacy again)
- sells the brand inside and out

The results of subsequent research by Barbour management demonstrate that the vast majority of employees believed that the change management program and values development process have directly contributed to recent business success.

Who are the most important communicators in the Barbour business?

As a relatively small business, and given Barbour's family heritage, the most impactful communicator is the MD. He sets the vision and strategic direction for the business.

Internally, however, every employee is an important communicator and is valued as such. It is essential that information is shared between departments in order for people to be able to do their jobs.

The Marketing department communicates the Barbour vision to consumers via advertising, PR, direct mail, point of sale, window displays and web communications but Barbour employees are clearly critical to whether that communication amounts to anything.

Line managers are an integral part of relaying information to employees and looping feedback back into the consciousness of the decision-makers. Line managers communicate the strategy of the business to their people in a way that makes sense for local audiences and they ensure that the objectives of the business are consistent with the brand and its values.

By improving the brand perception generally, recruitment is easier as potential recruits are already familiar with the brand and are excited by the opportunity to join it. Recently, Barbour HQ have noticed an increase in the number of speculative CVs, and this can be attributed, they believe, to the increased profile of the brand through PR and advertising in the media leading to a heightened awareness of the brand.

Brand values are an integral part of the performance reviews which take place for all employees every six months. They form part of the setting of individual and departmental objectives, and the competency framework, which demonstrates appropriate behavior, is directly linked to the values. Achievement of results is at the center of the brand values.

However, it is not the brand alone that retains people – the brand is in many respects a product of the culture that is created and it's that culture which determines employee satisfaction. Good working conditions, the opportunity to contribute, stability and a feeling of making a difference all help to empower the employee and make retention easier.

For example, in Barbour's factory 90% of the production workforce have been with Barbour for over a year, with a large proportion of employees having over ten years' service. That's unusual for a production business. It's a similar story in many other departments.

In a 2007 survey, 84% said that they were proud to work at Barbour and 88% were committed to work for the company. Applying the Brand Energy Investment Indicator, the current analysis of employees is shown in Figure 34.

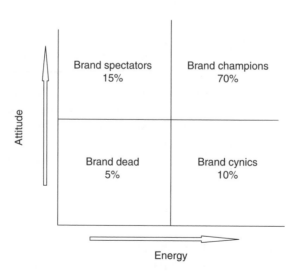

FIGURE 34 **Brand Energy Investment model**

Compare that with the survey results where you work.

One of the priorities of Barbour's change management program is to develop employees based on the foundation provided by the Barbour values and to enable them to confidently take ownership and responsibility (the most evolved form of employee engagement). This has two very clear benefits:

■ there is a positive environment and culture within the company because each employee knows where they stand and employees live by a common set of agreed values and standards
■ the way Barbour is perceived externally and how Barbour does business is a product of and is consistent with those values

The aim is that Barbour is a brand that is professional and personable at all times and one that people consequently want to do business with.

The Barbour brand undoubtedly benefits from being a household name. Most people when asked will have heard of a Barbour waxed jacket and know that it's a classic, upmarket, quality product. It's a reputation that has had to be earned. This gives Barbour an advantage over some of their competitors who do not have Barbour's legacy, heritage, reputation or history.

As Sue Newton, PR Manager, states: *"You should never underestimate how important the trust is between company and consumer and how long it takes to build up or how quickly it can be destroyed."*

Barbour's "magic dust" is clearly their product range. Their proposition is unique in that Barbour customers choose to wear the brand for so many different reasons – whether it's for shooting or equestrian activity, working in the country or slipping a quilted jacket over a suit in the city. Their products are both practical and functional and convey a sense of classicism linked to their target customer base and associated pursuits.

Yet the products are nothing without the consistent adherence to the underlying principles that the company was founded on and which are never knowingly compromised – those of durability, fitness for purpose and attention to detail. As Sue says,

This commitment to quality in practice, the fact that our classic wax jackets are still made in South Shields and the company's customer service promise whereby wax jackets can be returned to be rewaxed or reproofed

at any time, help to make employees proud to work for the company. And the way in which proud employees bring those values to life in their inter-actions with each other and customers makes Barbour employees unique. Barbour products may be the magic dust, the USP, but Barbour employees are our "dust sparklers." There is a pride and professionalism and many employees see it as much more than a job. Just like many Barbour custom-ers talk of their jackets as being old friends, many employees will always go the extra mile because they believe in the brand so passionately, which is why I prefer to talk about our people in plural rather than single out any one employee for special brand ambassador status.

Barbour's customer services team, for example, are consistently praised by customers for their helpfulness and friendliness. These are just some of the comments in a weekly customer post bag:

Your staff are a credit to you. May I also comment on the kindness and helpfulness of the ladies in your customer services department? You are one of very few companies with whom I deal that it can be said that deal-ing with you is a pleasure.

MH, London

Thank you for your excellent after sales service. The repair is of the highest standard and the re-proofing makes the jacket look new. I will in the future not fail to recommend Barbour to friends and colleagues.

TS, Tynemouth

Your service is right out of "dreamland" and far beyond what any cus-tomer would or could expect. It seems completely inadequate just to say thank you – but – again many thanks.

GC, Epsom

Of course they love to receive compliments, who doesn't?, but they also love to share stories about great on-brand behavior at workshops and in their regular internal communication in order to celebrate team achievements and create an appreciative atmosphere. It's not unknown, for example, for employees to volunteer to customize jackets for free for customers who, through no fault of the company, have been wrongly sold garments that don't fit because the customer has unique needs.

In April 2008, the entire global office network happily came together to celebrate the centenary of the original Barbour catalog. Brand champions were nominated from each office from the UK to the US to Germany to coordinate the celebration activities. It became a Barbour jamboree which, as one employee commented, *"was fantastically reassuring that we were working together as a team towards a common purpose."*

In 2007, Barbour teamed up with the Playtex Moonwalk to help promote the event, which raises money for breast cancer. The girls in the factory divided themselves into teams, and in their own time each team designed a bra using spare material, zips and buttons. With the girls choosing to model their creations themselves, the bras were then judged by those legendary Barbour brand champions Dame Margaret and her daughter, Helen Barbour. The winning bra was sent down to London to be auctioned for charity.

Barbour is a brand that is true to its legacy yet has moved with and adapted to the times to the point that a range which was exclusively for men until five or so years ago is now sported by 20-something female popstars like Lily Allen and gentleman farmers alike.

FIGURE 35 **Some of the Barbour brand champions sporting their Moonwalk bras**

According to Chris Sanderson cofounder of international trend consultancy The Future Laboratory, the revival of the Barbour is part of the trend for authenticity:

> *It's about products built to last, and which have a style and identity of* their *own without swamping yours: a Barbour's waxed cotton exudes sustainability and lived-in individuality.*
> *For this generation, it's quite a discovery. It's a complete change from the street and casual sportswear and nylon they are used to.* ("Why the Barbour is Suddenly So Rock n Roll," *Daily Mail,* March 2008)

By embracing:

- product
- people
- process

their approach to brand management is simple. Champions abound at Barbour in various guises. But the Barbour story isn't so much a brand development odyssey undertaken by any one individual. It has been and continues to be a family and extended community affair. Clearly the energy and initiative shown by Barbour's founding fathers have been perpetuated by the immediate and wider family of brand ambassadors who care deeply about the brand values. They have overcome the slings and arrows of the fashion industry to take the Barbour brand development journey into new territories and fresh generations of customers and staff alike, who, in turn, have become the latest of a long line of advocates of the Barbour brand.

TOP CASE STUDY TIPS:

- use your legacy to anchor the brand but not constrain it
- if you have senior brand champions use them well but ensure that the values they represent are owned by everyone
- keep your communication and engagement strategy simple
- ensure your change plan is rooted in the brand values and links to the ongoing narrative conveying the development of the brand
- make the most of customer advocacy to reinforce a positive culture

- engaging, integrated brands build trust, enhance reputation and create advocacy
- brands that engage their colleagues around their *values* close the gap between what they say and do through how they say it and how they do it

PERSPECTIVES ACROSS INDUSTRIES

The core thesis explored here is that brands are predominantly behavioral, and consequently any brand management program or initiative should involve a collaboration between the internal and external custodians of the brand to serve the brand communities. Brand champions are essentially the voluntary, workaday people who ensure that the organization keeps the promises it makes to customers, corporate partners, colleagues and society. It is essential, therefore, that employees are engaged with the brand in the context of the legacy, business direction, objectives and challenges – the story of where the organization has been and is going.

In the autumn of 2008, the UK Secretary of State for Business commissioned a report into employee engagement and to report on its potential benefits for companies, organizations and individuals. This has since become known as the *MacLeod Report*, named after the person fortunate enough to have obtained the commission and undertaken the analysis.

The report concludes that there is an unequivocal business case for employee engagement:

We believe that if employee engagement and the principles that lie behind it were more widely shared, if the potential that resides in the country's workforce was more fully unleashed, we could see a step change in workplace performance and in employee well-being, for the considerable benefit of UK plc. (David MacLeod, Letter to delegates, Employee Engagement and Employer Branding Conference, September 2009)

Fine words. The MacLeod report makes a very strong case for employee engagement being reliant upon:

- a strong strategic narrative from the leaders
- engaging, facilitating and empowering line managers (or ceos in my language)

- employees having a voice and being consulted and listened to
- behavior within the organization being consistent with values and conveying integrity as a result

The breadth and depth of support that the findings have attracted has considerable implications for my notion of a joined-up approach to brand management. The *MacLeod Report* may be UK centric, but consider these sound bites from brand champions drawn from a select group of high-profile international brands, who presented at the same event:

> **The power of brand is unmistakeable,** *because talented people can choose who they want to work for and, increasingly, people think about their experience as a customer and make assumptions about what it would be like to work for that company. At Iceland our challenge as a value-based retailer is that people may perceive us as offering a "bargain basement" employee experience. ... Our challenge in HR is to ensure every "touch point" for prospective and existing employees is positive and consistent. To do this we group HR activity around three key elements:*
>
> *1. Feels like Family*
> *2. Keeping Things Simple*
> *3. Something for Everyone*
>
> *Our People Plan brings these to life.*
>
> Susan Yell,
> HR, Iceland

Susan made a very strong case for the role of HR working with Marketing to develop the Iceland brand from the inside out.

> *QBE is one of the world's largest insurance companies. In 2008, following a restructure and rebrand...we consolidated six brands and 13 business units into eight underwriting divisions. ... We needed to raise brand awareness.* **To build external brand effectively, it is vital to first have a sound employee understanding of an organisation's values, aims and strengths** *...we adopted* **an inside-out approach to brand building.**
>
> Samantha Children,
> European Operations, QBE

*In the long run, the only key to success is having talented people who become **passionate ambassadors for your business**...we've been focusing on three areas:*

1. attraction
2. selection
3. engagement

The driver connecting them is your employer branding promise.

Job Mensink,
Global Head of Employer Branding, Royal Philips

*The employee brand proposition is being applied internally across a number of **touchpoints on the employee journey.** These include:*

- *the recruitment process*
- *the role of the line manager*
- *compensation and benefits*
- *training and development.*

Madeleine Abdoh,
Head, Employee Brand, BBC

Interestingly, Job stresses employee advocacy at Philips, while Madeleine used the journey metaphor extensively and made a compelling case for recognizing the line manager as a pivot point for the perpetuation of the brand in an organization that has had significant brand management challenges in recent times.

*Cisco Systems has a vision to change the way we work, live, play and learn. Realising this vision and **achieving our brand goals requires total employee engagement across the globe.** Our European people strategy, known as i-Count@Cisco, is fundamental in driving our ability to discover, build and enable people. It uses a Five People Pillar Framework:*

1. our company
2. our values
3. leaders and team
4. development and opportunity
5. contribution and reward

Each pillar is led by an executive board member and HR executive.

Mark Hamberlin,
Senior Director, Human Resources, Cisco Europe

The rhetoric in Cisco is engagement and enabling led rather than alignment and management focused. This is reinforced in Sabine Schauer's strong rhetoric about the importance of brand management from within by sustaining trust:

> *A strong corporate identity is crucial for economic success, especially during a downturn. "**Trust** is the most important capital of a worldwide brand," the American investor Warren Buffet is quoted as saying. **Trust** can only be built up if the internal audience, namely the employees, are convinced and stand behind the brand...**people breathe life into brands** and sharpen their profile in the face of our competitors. Our focus has been to win over employees as valuable supporters and multipliers. Reinforcing the corporate brand in the minds of employees is the decisive factor underlying the success in promoting a specific image or reputation with external stakeholders.*

> Sabine Schauer,
> Head of Corporate Communications, EMEA, Henkel CEE GmbH

> *Being a change agent or engagement leader means being involved, feeling empowered to speak up and actually say what many are thinking but are unwilling to say out loud.*

> Frederick Wittock,
> Senior Director, Global R&D Communication, Johnson & Johnson PRD

These cross-industry soundbites from senior brand champions representing a range of international organizations help to reinforce many of the key themes we've explored together. This is not the "nice to have" rhetoric of the economic boom time but the "must have" logic of senior executives who recognize the route to employee engagement and the link between advocacy and brand development. The final case study brings these themes together in a way that has generated external validation of brand-building efforts on an exceptional scale in an industry and an operating environment that has not been without controversy in recent times.

DEVELOPING A BRAND CHAMPION CULTURE AT BRITISH GAS

With 27,000 employees and a presence in over 12million British homes, British Gas is one of the most well-known and well-recognized brands in the UK today.

Despite a turbulent energy market and global recessionary worries 2009 was a year of significant achievement for the company, with improvements in customer service and price competitiveness leading to a growth in customer accounts and strong financial performance.

The company is a key part of Centrica, an integrated energy company operating predominately in the UK and North America. As a strong vote of confidence in its improved performance and longer-term strategy, Centrica has placed the growth of British Gas at the heart of its new strategic priorities, with an aim of *"leading the transition to low carbon homes and businesses."*

As Dave Hughes, Internal Communications Business Partner, explains, the British Gas story hasn't always been one of success, however.

> *It wasn't so long ago that customer satisfaction levels were rock bottom and the company was experiencing significant system and billing issues after a difficult IT implementation – a period which had a huge impact on the way that the public perceive British Gas.*

Following a change in leadership, over the past three years the company has been on a major transformation program aimed at addressing these service issues and arresting a decline in public perception of the brand. This process was initiated by splitting the company into smaller, focused businesses and tasking each one to fix the basics and to put the customer back at the heart of the company. It's an intimacy and community approach favored by brands like Virgin and Google.

A key part of the strategy has been the role of *listening* to customers and employees in equal measure about areas where improvements can be made, and involving these groups in ongoing improvements.

Individual business units like British Gas Cardiff understand that this process of talking, listening, acting on feedback and involving people in the changes has been critical to kick-start the improvements needed in customer service and brand perception. It was clear to the British Gas leaders that their heritage brand associations had to be carefully managed if they were to compete with funkier brands in a demanding and rapidly changing market.

The Cardiff office is one of six British Gas energy contact centers. It employs 1200 people and handles roughly 4.5million customer contacts a year for over 2.3million customers.

An innovative mix of leadership, training and internal communication strategies have been used to create a unique culture that's now driving a more customer-centric, modern and personal experience for its customers. The result is a highly engaged workforce delivering first-class customer service, rightly earning British Gas Cardiff the prestigious title of European Call Centre of the Year in 2009. Call centers may not always attract the most favorable press, so external validation of British Gas Cardiff's customer service credentials was very welcome and a source of significant pride for the staff.

The heart of the challenge in British Gas Cardiff has been moving people away from a sales culture and into the mindset of putting themselves in the customer's shoes to get under the surface of how different customers want to be dealt with: a shift from sales focus to empathy and old-fashioned customer service.

A series of innovative training programs have been delivered to support this. Entitled "Look Who's...," these programs have been focused on improving the customer experience across different contact types.

"Look Who's Calling," for example, focused on inbound customer calls, encouraging people to identify customers' personality types (based on a simplified Myers Briggs), and helping them adapt their behavior to different personality types. It clearly works.

Following a rollout that used actors to coach people in how to apply the theory, the program has been sustained via a range of means, including communications support and best practice case studies/customer stories. The program has yielded impressive returns from both a customer satisfaction and an inter-team perspective.

"Look Who's Writing" was the next stage of this development program, helping to create a more personal and intimate tone of voice in written communications. This was built on the success of "Look Who's Calling," but helped people understand how they could introduce key brand attributes into their correspondence to bring a more personal, customer focused approach to communication.

These kinds of initiatives have been well received by people in British Gas Cardiff. In an interview with three Contact Centre Brand Agents from British Gas Cardiff, Kath James, Louise Clark and Daniel Jones, the training programs as well as the other initiatives were discussed.

Louise begins:

The "Look Who's …" initiatives have been groundbreaking for us as a business. We're trusted to be ourselves. You don't have to be this scripted, insincere, robotic call center person anymore. We're able to adapt to the people we speak with now, whoever that might be. And it's helped us recognize that we're all unique people with unique needs, and call on the various skills we've got to make sure that our customers leave happy.

FIGURE 36   **Brand champions in action at British Gas**

Louise clearly feels more empowered and consequently more engaged.

Engaging people in the business goals and strategy has also been a key step in British Gas Cardiff's development strategy. As well as creating a two-way communications framework that incorporates monthly manager briefings, intranet news, regular leadership blogs and an ideas scheme, helping people understand the strategy and how to bring it to life is critical. Regular face-to-face strategy sessions with the leadership team are well received.

Kath commented:

The quarterly sessions – the Touchpoint events – are superb. They help you understand what's been happening for the last three months, and what's coming up in the next quarter. The managers are out and about explaining the plans to you, sharing the vision, explaining what we're aiming for and what we need to do. It makes you feel part of it – more of a team effort than a "them and us" culture, which so many businesses are like. There's no shocks and surprises anymore either. You know what's coming, you feel more involved and you understand the journey we're going on.

But the company also employs more innovative approaches when required. In 2009 the company introduced a significant organizational change – which resulted in the introduction of a new shared vision and values, as well as a new set of business priorities and its Brand Promise. This provided a very real communications challenge and the requirement for a special approach.

To achieve this, British Gas Cardiff deployed an innovative engagement program, "All on the Same Page," that helped people understand the changes, and bring them to life in their everyday roles. Following pre-engagement sessions with team managers, senior managers, and engagement representatives, the program culminated in a series of three-hour "Touchpoint" events for all colleagues, featuring playful and highly interactive sessions that brought energy and involvement to the changes. The sessions were task-based, and used a number of interventions to help embed the changes:

■ a creative "big picture" graphic was used to depict the direction and changes involved. This approach turned the "strategy" into an analogy for the changes and became a useful tool for the managers to use in storytelling

- a special extended section on brand asked groups to explore the British Gas Brand Promise ("Count on Us to Look After Your World") and compare the British Gas brand with other companies. Attendees discussed their responsibilities in representing British Gas and were asked to consider their customers' worlds.

There was a sense of optimism in the exercise, that the company could start comparing the British Gas brand with brands like O2 or Tesco – top table brands – and encouraging people to consider what might be possible by working together, building on the company's heritage and existing market position.

- as part of these events, groups were also given an exercise to create two-minute YouTube style films with Flip-cams and props to show how they're currently living the British Gas values. Finished products ranged from the obvious to the truly innovative, and a shortlist of the best videos was shown on the intranet after the session, where people could vote for their favorites.

- the sessions ended with blue-sky thinking on just what could be possible. A "Star Wall" ideas session encouraged individuals to put forward ideas for making change happen, pulling together over 1000 ideas that have fed through into the ongoing ideas scheme.

FIGURE 37 **Involvement is key to engagement**

One-off events are never enough, however. Creating a culture where people can continuously commit themselves to the opportunities available has been critical.

Dan comments:

I've been here three years, my longest serving job. I like the amount of variety. I started doing one role, but within a year I could do a few different things. If you give 100%, the company gives you 100% back. Having accountability and ownership is important, and if I wasn't treated like an adult, I'd be gone. Things have definitely changed. Before I felt like a number, like a sheep, but now all of us are willingly playing our part.

Louise carries on with this ownership theme:

I came here as a stop-gap from University, but the company provides the right incentives, the right career paths, the right opportunities, and I've found myself applying for something you never thought you'd apply for – like the Reach program [career development program]. There are so many engaging initiatives going on at any one time. It's one of the things we do really well.

This strategy of "self-selection" is critical. The British Gas office in Cardiff is currently reviewing its shift pattern – traditionally a challenging activity. But instead of this presenting a challenge, people in British Gas Cardiff are actually motivated by the change. They understand the business requirement for changing the shift patterns, and a working party of volunteers has been formed to recommend the shape of the new shifts.

Kath elaborates:

I've never worked anywhere where the management cares so much about how you feel. They want to know about what you're doing. They care about how you feel about coming into work to stop people being off sick; they want to have a discussion about it. Not just to keep the figures down, but trying to find ways of working around the problems. They're always trying to find ways to appeal to you, rather than setting something for you to be frightened of – coming up with different ideas. I've never worked anywhere where they care so much about the people; they want to know what you think so that it can become a better place to work for everyone.

Providing people with a voice has been critical. For example, an office move was used as an opportunity to leave behind aspects of the old culture and adopt new practices and ways of working, and the British Gas Cardiff ideas forum is well used, receiving 350–400 ideas a month, another sign of a truly engaged community. On a smaller, more tactical level, people are treated like adults. Free toast, cereal, fruit and hot drinks are readily available across the office, replacing vending machines that cost more to maintain and in the loss of goodwill than they generate. Again this is a best practice shared at the likes of Google, Orange, the best advertising agencies, McKinseys and eBay.

So what have all these changes resulted in? Well the signs are that all these elements are working. In 2009, employee engagement scores rose by 12% and NPS (customer satisfaction) scores were up by 483% across 2009 in general.

Louise comments:

We've got a long way to go, but it's changing. Now it's in our gift to change people's perceptions of British Gas. It's the courses, the training and the support that we've had that helps us do that. We can be more personal and honest and straightforward with customers. Customers are starting to understand that when there's a problem, there are other things outside of our control that can have caused it to happen – things like metering, for example. They're doing that because we're being honest, we're not hiding behind technical words and phrases or insincere promises and buck passing any more. It's very fresh . . . still corporate and business-like, but more friendly and tailored to the customer. There's still a long way to go, but we're definitely more human than we have been before.

Instead of being a number, we're people with a career path and a part to play in the business. We're doing the same thing with our customers; we're turning them from the reference numbers they had become and back into real people. Now we can picture a customer as a person – someone who likes to walk his dog at night, someone with two kids; someone that you think you know.

Note the absence of prescriptive language and the focus on engaging, empowering, trusting and liberating approaches summed up in the words *"we're definitely more human than we have been before."*

How ridiculous it is that organizations can perpetuate practices that apparently dehumanize their people. Yet it happens.

Brand champions clearly abound at British Gas Cardiff, supported by a deliberate program of employee focused engagement initiatives and a comprehensive culture change program. The brand has been transformed and the results speak for themselves, as British Gas brand advocates from across the four Cs of customers, colleagues, corporate partners and social communities attest.

British Gas Cardiff's roll of honor to date
- European Call Centre of the Year 2009
- Best Improvement Strategy in Europe 2009
- Best Centre to Work for in Europe 2009
- Customer Service Back-Office Team of the Year 2009 at the National Customer Service Awards
- Welsh Call Centre Award for People Development 2009
- Welsh Call Centre Award for Team Manager of the Year 2009 – Roy Werrett
- Welsh Call Centre Award for Excellence in a Support Team – Andrea Lee's Commercial & Marketing Team
- Call Centre Management Association Team Manager of the Year 2009 – Ami Campbell
- *Sunday Times* 2010 Big Ranking – 22 (Best Companies Evaluation) (British Gas)
- *Financial Times* – Great Places to Work 2010 – 30th (British Gas)

The judges' comments at the European awards were:

- ***Best Center to Work For*** *– The winner is a center that is slick, consistent, with great initiatives and has a real focus on the sharing of best practice and winning over both the hearts and minds of the team.*
- ***Best Improvement Strategy*** *– A strong winner that delivered positively across the board. Clear objectives, excellent planning, and exemplary delivery ...*
- ***European Call Center of the Year*** *– A strong performer, on the up and heading for real success...*

Praise from visiting companies

My contact with you and your team at British Gas in Cardiff has been a delightful experience with warmth from your people and very energetic approach to improve their performance especially in service. My team that joined me on the visit to Cardiff were impressed with the environment and the people and came away inspired with many ideas to implement back at Autoglass.

Bill Kalyan,
Head of Customer Contact Centre, Autoglass

We feel we have been on the journey with you – and it has been an absolute pleasure. You all deserve the awards and accolades for your passion, focus, hard work and sheer persistence! It must be remembered that you have achieved all this during a time of price increases and recession which has certainly made the hurdles bigger. We are very proud to have worked with you during the last 20 months and know you will continue to go from strength to strength.

Jill Dean,
Client Services Director, PowerTrain

It's always been a pleasure to work with the team at Premier Energy. The organization is full of people who care deeply about customers, are clear in their vision of service excellence and demonstrate the courage and creativity to innovate.

Adam Walton,
Vice President, CallMiner

TOP CASE STUDY TIPS:

- ensure that you build engagement activity from the ground upward
- involving people not only sends out an empowering message but most people learn much more readily when they're engaged in activity and are obviously trusted
- brand engagement programs have to be tailored to the culture and be led by champions of the culture
- external endorsement and advocacy helps build pride and sustain a brand champion culture

I'm a well-publicized critic of the call center model. But I can think of a host of organizations with similar call centers to that of British Gas Cardiff which could transform their businesses and brands overnight if they only took one half of the best practices from this case study on board. Creating a brand engaged culture obviously pays dividends.

Interestingly, when speaking with Dave and his team, they don't single out any particularly heroic individuals for extra high praise. That's how it tends to be inside the great brands: the heroic behavior has become systemic, the way of the culture.

As I've hopefully illustrated throughout these case studies, the link between brand strength and a well-defined and complementary internal culture is undeniable. Where strong cultures exist, reinforcing the brand rather than undermining the brand promise, the brand superheroes are so common it seems wrong to single them out by asking them to don a funny outfit.

Despite the implication in the title that brands are underpinned by superheroes, I've hopefully illustrated that potential brand superheroes exist everywhere and that most brand champions are ordinary people looking to make the most of their workaday experience. In the process they become brand advocates and it becomes infectious. They spend a lot of time at work and instinctively want to make a difference and want to care about what they do. Managers and strategists often lose touch with that very basic and very human fact.

Brands don't survive or thrive on the back of beauty parades involving a carefully groomed few. Whether your brand champions come in the understated and empathetic guise of Mel at CFS or the entrepreneurial form of Gil at Christie's, have the gift of the gab of the MD at NITB, the youthful exuberance of the British Gas teams or the fun loving, down to earth approach of the Barbour ladies, great brands rely upon brand values being consistently and passionately applied throughout, from the back office to the customer service frontline. Whatever form your brand journey takes, be it heroic or mundane, extroverted or understated, it requires a well thought through and defined program of change ranging from a clear and compelling story to provide context and focus through to authentic engagement initiatives aimed at involving, motivating, liberating and sustaining employee initiative.

PART 6

BRAND ENGAGEMENT AND THE BRAND ENGAGED ORGANIZATION – THE FUTURE

There are still persistent critics who decry the very notion of brand and who question its relevance to employees in particular. It's my experience that the commentators who hold those views usually have too narrow a definition of brand and find it hard to see beyond the logo, font, strap line and color palette.

I have no doubt, however, that brand is a powerful and unifying route to sustainable employee engagement. It is still a largely underutilized asset. There's also no doubt in my mind that employee engagement is absolutely critical to an organization's performance and that the brand can and should be a powerful unifying force. It's difficult to argue with the assertion that, however automated the business model, or however innovative the product range, it is only through employees that organizations can keep the promises they make to their external stakeholders. Brand engaged organizations are high-performing organizations.

Employees or colleagues are only one of the many communities an organization's brand needs to engage with if the organization is to sustain the reputation of its brand. A truly brand engaged organization takes a joined-up approach to positively influence stakeholder relations.

THE FOUR Cs

- community – social responsibility, good neighbor
- colleagues – great employer, recruitment and retention
- customer – experience, satisfaction, innovation
- corporate partners – investor and value chain, governance and sustainability

It's no longer possible to control stakeholder perceptions with silo-specific PR. The stakeholder communities are converging all the time. Boundaries are blurring on the back of:

- a broader base of shareholding
- colleagues increasingly becoming aware of their power as consumers as well as employees
- the liberation of customer choice and mobility through online purchasing
- the increasing use of electronic communication and the power, reach, unpredictability and response time of social media

Engaging, integrated brands build trust, enhance their reputation and create advocacy.

Reams have been written about the power of brand as a route to attracting customer and consumer loyalty. It's time the proverbial penny dropped that the key to sustainability and reputation management rests with the internal stakeholder market and that brand management should be as much of a concern for the HR department as Marketing.

It clearly follows that engaged employees who consistently act as brand advocates by championing the brand values and delivering consistently in line with the goals of the business are worth their weight in gold. The ultimate measure of colleague engagement levels is their level of advocacy for your brand. Rather than spending a fortune on bi-annual, hugely expensive, often mis-directed employee satisfaction surveys, executive teams would be better off simply asking their colleagues:

- would you promote us amongst your friends and family as a responsible company?
- would you recommend us to your friends and family as a great place to work?
- would you recommend our products and services to your friends and family?
- would you promote us amongst your friends and family as a good business to deal with/invest in?

Champion brands understand the power of advocacy and usually take the trouble to measure it. The ultimate level of advocacy is that displayed by the role model brand champion, wherever they're found and whatever they look and sound like. As we've seen, true brand champions are much more likely to be representatives of the Everyman community than management elected, conscribed or aligned corporate courtesans.

Brand champions are largely the product of nurture rather than nature, which is great news for brand managers. It means we can all do it and can all play a part in creating the conditions in which brand champions thrive. By recognizing the importance of employee engagement, leadership development and creating a sustainable, constructive culture, brand managers, wherever they may be located, can transform customer perceptions of their brand.

People power is the key. But it means crossing the threshold of the Marketing and HR departments, consulting, involving and engaging people, role modeling values and focusing on authentic communication. It also calls for real and lasting partnerships between the external and internal facing parts of the business to ensure consistency and to bring rigor and inspiration and authenticity to the process. More likely than not, until brand management is recognized as a truly holistic discipline, it also requires internal partnerships to secure the investment required to create an internal culture in which brand engagement is prioritized and nurtured.

Equipping, informing and upskilling brand champions is obviously important. But even if you accept that this means ensuring that everyone keeps your brand promises, as we've seen it need not be expensive. On the contrary, it not only pays for itself but also delivers exponentially high returns for the effort invested. The alternative can be extremely costly. And what price reputation?

If brand engagement activity linked to leveraging the power of brand champions is related to the cost of acquiring and retaining staff and customers alike, the legal cost of nonconformance or the opportunity cost of missed opportunities, there's undeniably a clear business case for making the investment in the behavioral side of brand management. This is especially true when you consider the price so many brands have paid and still pay for doing the wrong thing or, worse still, doing nothing.

Brand engagement through unleashing the power of brand champions is highly infectious, especially when your superheroes are encouraged to be themselves at work.

So what's stopping you?

EPILOGUE

THE ONGOING QUEST TO DISCOVER BRAND CHAMPIONS

Back in 2003, I set up Interbrand's first internal brand engagement practice. In doing so I combined the methodologies of one of the premier brand agencies with the leading internal communication and change management consultancy. The aim was to provide holistic brand development support and build brands from the inside out.

When I set up the Bring Yourself 2 Work Fellowship, the goal was to take this approach a step further. I wanted to explore the relationship between the individual and the brand they work for by helping organizations develop brand engagement strategies that are predominantly employee focused and include effective approaches to employee engagement, culture development, leadership development and change management, bridging the gap between the internal and external representations of the brand. Many of the brands and the people featured in this book are testimony to that approach.

In 2010 the brand landscape is changing faster than ever before. Following the ongoing liberation of communication as a result of emerging media and a number of high-profile brand disasters, which were to some extent forecast in *Brand Engagement*, consumers of brands are becoming increasingly discerning, demanding unprecedented levels of transparency and authenticity. The gap between what a brand delivers and what it promises is under increasing scrutiny from all stakeholder groups, and at the forefront of this critique are employees.

Traditional communication channels are converging. The explosion of social media and media-savvy society demands more sophisticated approaches to how brands communicate with their consumers, communities, colleagues and investors alike. It demands at least as much flexibility from trusted advisers, the bulk of whom still cater to either the external or occasionally internal brandscape.

Even with the proliferation of internal communication functions, the internal communication profession is fragmented, with wide fault lines between strategists and message managers, and, with very few notable exceptions, internal communication has not managed to secure the place at the top table predicted by some. Despite the growing weight of evidence suggesting the need for joined-up thinking when it comes to brand management, there's still very little partnership thinking within organizations, and the internal communities are suffering the most.

Pushing messages into the market is not enough to differentiate your brand. The leading brands of the future will be the brands that innovate in how they engage with their full range of stakeholders. The future is less about what a brand promises than about what a brand delivers; more about how it expresses itself and how it ensures a consistent brand experience across all touch points. This will require an alternative approach to how organizations organize themselves.

Never has there been a greater need for a flexible and joined-up approach to brand management, yet the departmental boundaries that create functional silos are being reinforced. External agencies and consultancies have become even more fragmented, commoditizing products and services to reinforce and protect the functional bastions and budgets, and in many cases deepening the problem.

This business model needs to be broken up. We need to tear down the walls within organizations and agencies if we're to create truly engaged enterprises that deliver innovation in brand expression and experience.

My next venture aims to take brand engagement to the next level. Having previously united the external and internal brand development methodologies via the Bring Yourself 2 Work Fellowship, I'm now uniting the approaches of the two leading marcomms agencies by joining forces with Sean Trainor, founder of uber engagement and former practice leader for WPP's The Brand Union.

Recognizing the undeniable link between individual brand advocacy, brand champions and brand performance, we have launched TBT Engaged. We aim to provide the best advice for enterprises that are looking for enlightenment in their journeys to becoming leading brands.

With an ongoing zeal for reinforcing the strong link between individual brand advocates, brand champions and brand performance, we have launched the TBTEngaged – Brand Champions Quest. We're seeking brand-engaged or champion brands that epitomize the holistic approach to brand development I've explored here.

We also aim to hold an annual conference of brand champions and to present annual awards celebrating the rounded, sustainable, leading brands and the people who make them great. We will very gladly celebrate these role models in the next book in this series, so if you know one, you are one or just suspect that the "cut of the jib" of a colleague suggests that, secretly, they are one, don't be shy and do drop us a line.

Find out more about the Brand Champions Quest on our website, www.tbtengaged.com, or contact me direct using ian@by2w.co.uk or ian@tbtengaged.com.

ACKNOWLEDGEMENTS

Given the subject matter of this book, it seems appropriate first and foremost to recognize the contributions of the unsung heroes out there who, in good times and especially bad, undertake the largely thankless task of creating and sustaining the brands they work for. I've managed to unmask a few here, but to the very many more, whoever you are, whatever you look like and wherever you work: Keep going; your colleagues and customers need you.

This book would not have been possible without the contributions, insights, challenges and suggestions of a special group of people. Particular thanks are extended to the following folk, all brand champions in their own right, who provided their encouragement and support and co-created a number of the case studies: the mysterious Magnificent Seven, who generously gave of their time in return for little more than caffeine and buns, Kate Feather of PeopleMetrics (www. peoplemetrics.com), Roberto F. Assunto, Jose Antonio Flores and Tim Stokes, Gillian Magee, Brenda Murphy and Kathryn Thomson, Sue Newton, Dave Hughes, Mel Cartwright, Rob Woolley, Richard Lewis, Anna Farmery, Wayne Turmel (aka the Cranky Middle Manager, www. crankymiddlemanager.com), Dave Reilly and Sean Trainor. Thanks also to Lisa Marsala, Interbrand Group Communications Director, for permission to cite the Best Global Brands research, and to Deborah Valentine and Katie Pattullo of Osney Media (www.osneymedia.com) for the extracts from *Employee Engagement Today* and the employee engagement conference.

Thank you to all the threshold guardians who gave permission to use the quotes and references that have helped to add context and colour to this work.

Last, but certainly not least, I extend my appreciation to the Palgrave Macmillan team, from the designers through to the copyeditors, who collaborated on this work and helped produce this and the prequel,

Brand Engagement. Long may the Palgrave Macmillan brand prosper despite these challenging times for the industry.

Every effort has been made to trace all copyright holders, but if any have been inadvertently overlooked the publishers will be pleased to make the necessary arrangements at the first opportunity.

BIBLIOGRAPHY*

Preliminaries

Interbrand website http://www.interbrand.com/en/best-global-brands/Best-Global-Brands-2010.aspx

Part 1

Buckingham, Ian P (2007), *Brand Engagement*, Palgrave Macmillan

Campbell, Joseph (2004), *Pathways to Bliss: Mythology and Personal Transformation*, New World Library

Campbell, Joseph (July 28, 2008), *The Hero with a Thousand Faces*, 3rd edition, Fontana

The Incredibles (2005), Walt Disney Home Entertainment

Vogler, Christopher (1998), *The Writer's Journey*, 1st edition, Michael Wiese Productions

Woods, David (18 June 2010), HR Forum: You have to move quickly to get staff buy-in after a merger, says Santander's HR boss, *HR Magazine*, Haymarket, www.hrmagazine.co.uk

Part 2

Barrett, Richard (2006), *Building a Values-Driven Organisation*, Butterworth-Heinemann

Barrow, Simon (2005), *The Employer Brand*, John Wiley & Sons

Browne, John (2010), *Beyond Business: An Inspirational Memoir from a Visionary Leader*, W&N

Bolchover, David (November 4, 2005) *The Living Dead: Switched Off, Zoned Out – The Shocking Truth about Office Life*, Capstone

Buckingham, Ian P (2007), *Brand Engagement*, Palgrave Macmillan

Buckingham, Ian, Trainor, Sean (2010), *Flying the Flag; blog post CIPR Inside*, http://ciprinside.wordpress.com/2010/05/28/flying-the-flag-half-mast/

Cockerell, Lee (2009), *Creating Magic: 10 Common Sense Leadership Strategies from a Life at Disney*, Vermilion

Cummings, Jonathan and Richard Groom (2008), *Branding Inside Out: The Pret a Manger Story*, Capstone

Gresh, Lois H. and Weinberg, R. (2004), *The Science of Supervillains*, John Wiley & Sons

Ind, Nicholas (2007*), Living the Brand, How to Transform Every Member of Your Organization into a Brand Champion*, Kogan Page

Jackson, Tim (1994), *Inside Richard Branson's Business Empire*, HarperCollins

Jones, Quentin and Human Synergistics International (2006), *In Great Company: Unlocking the Secrets of Cultural Transformation*, Human Synergistics International

Mc Kevitt, Steve (2006), *City Slackers: Workers of the World... You are Wasting Your Time!* Cyan Books

Part 3

Chabon, Michael (2008), *The Amazing Adventures of Kavalier & Clay*, (Reissue) edition, Fourth Estate

Gresh, Lois and Robert Weinberg (2002), *The Science of Superheroes*, John Wiley & Sons

Irwin, William (2009), *Watchmen and Philosophy: A Rorschach Test*, John Wiley & Sons

Knowles, Chris (2007), *Our Gods Wear Spandex*, Red Wheel/Weiser

Morris, Tom and Morris, Matt (eds) (2006), *Superheroes and Philosophy: Truth, Justice, and The Socratic Way*, Open Court Publishing Co

Powell, Michael (2005), *The Superhero Handbook*, Sterling Publishing

Rosenburg, Robin (2008), *Psychology of Superheroes*, Ben Bella

Zander, Benjamin (2006), *The Art of Possibility: Practices in Leadership, Relationship and Passion*, Penguin

Part 4

Axelrod, Richard (2003), *Terms of Engagement: Changing the Way We Change Organizations*, Berrett-Koehler

Fischer, Hermann, (1991), *Romantic Verse Narrative: The History of a Genre* (European Studies in English Literature), Cambridge University Press

Hamilton, Edith (2000), *Mythology*, Little, Brown and Company

Morgan, Adam (2004), *The Pirate Inside: Building a Challenger Brand Culture Inside Yourself and Your Organizations*, John Wiley & Sons

Part 5

Arden, Paul (2003), *It's Not How Good You Are, It's How Good You Want To Be*, Phaidon

Arden, Paul (2006), *Whatever you Think, Think the Opposite*, Penguin

Pattullo, Katie (ed.) (2010), *Employee Engagement Today* Vol. 2.4, Osney Media

*Where possible, sources and references have been cited in the text for ease of use.

INDEX